THE
WHITE CORPSE HUSTLE:
A GUIDE FOR THE FLEDGLING VAMPIRE

DOCUMENTED BY
JOHN DIMES

LEMON PI BOOKS

For Count Gore,

and all the horror hosts all over the world

And most especially for the whimsy and wisdom of

George Clinton

And the late, great Douglas Adams

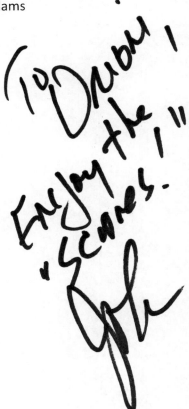

Lemon Pi First Edition

Introduction

By Dr. Horace Pike, Ph.D.,

Necropsychology, Psychology, Necroanthropology, Anthropology, Parapsychology

Firstly, I'd like to say I was quite jealous. Very, very jealous. Beyond envy, that I was contacted to merely introduce a book that _I_, by right of educational territory, should have translated. *Simply by right of educational territory.* My entire life's work has been devoted to the investigation of the paranormal, with an emphasis on the undead. Genus species: *Homo Non-silenti.* The undead of the variety including Zombies (*Homo Exitosus*), Hyper-Protoplasmic, Spectral Entities, Ghosts (*Homo Lemures*) if you will. And most especially Nosferatu, the Vampire (*Homo Montifera*).

The only reason Mr. Dimes has any legitimate claims on this property, is because of the nature of his acquaintance with one of the oldest living, let me rephrase, 'surviving' *Homo Montifera* in the country. It was by chance that the circumstances of this most uncommon dialogue with a human (*Homo Sapien*), and a Vampire (*Homo Montifera*), should occur.

Simply put: Mr. Dimes met Mr. Blassusos (made up name, obviously) at Point Direct Bar in Seattle, Washington.

Don't bother looking for the place. It has since shut down. Rodents, and such.

They 'discoursed' for the better part of three hours, over brandies, liqueurs, wines, and pretzels.

The subject matters? Everything contained in this book. But only after the initial discussion, which was: *Where to score weed.* Mr. Dimes hadn't a clue, simply because he was visiting for a week from Washington, D.C. He was immersing himself in the culture, in the hopes of possible relocation to Seattle. Blassusos hadn't a clue as to where one could effectively 'score' weed, seeing as he was also a recent visitor to America from Europe. If he were in England, where he has hailed for the past twenty-five years, he would have been able to score a couple of 'dashes' from a 'bloke' he knew in Bridport, Dorset. Blassusos explained that Seattle was merely a stopover until his next flight. He was on his way to a sunny weekend in San Francisco. His final destination: Hollywood. He was fascinated with stars, and the Hollywood 'machinery'.

Blassusos commented that Seattle felt right at home to him, however, with all it drear, and rain, so very much like England in the winter. But, the sky did show magnificently, when the sun challenged the Seattle clouds. And the mountains were certainly incredible. Like giant ice bergs in the middle of the city. But California beckoned.

Now if you've noticed, I put *'discoursed'* in italics, and quotations. There is a reason. A reason I would have noticed almost immediately were I in the company of these two gentlemen. Well, it was something that I noticed immediately simply because, when I finally had *my* encounter with Mr. Blassusos. . .*well*!

Five years prior to my encounter, I had a paper published on Ghost, Zombie, and Vampire Psychology, entitled, ***Vital Waters, Ruined Well: A Comprehensive Study of The Undead Mind***. I had, with great success, catalogued more than twenty-five cases of the mind-set of Ghosts, and as much as fifteen occurrences with Zombies. The cases of Ghosts were text book cases similar to that of M.P.D., Multiple Personalities, where the Spectral Entity, as does a facet/character of an MPD'S mind, would represent one event and one event only. Much like schizophrenics, or obsessive compulsives who are fixated on performing a fixed routine of patterned behavior. Of repeated actions. Washing the hands in lots of threes. Genuflecting seven times before every other trash can, and so forth. Ergo, *obsessive compulsive disorder*, with occasional moments of true clarity.

The zombie events--where I traveled as close as Patois country, the bayou areas of New Orleans, Louisiana, to the far-flung territory of *vodu* practices, Haiti--were, at best, static. The data compiled from these zombies (*Homo Exitosus)*, exhibited minds in various states of decay. Or *tabula rasa*. The conversations consisted primarily of mumbled, monosyllabic ramblings, really. Incessant demands for 'mother,' 'rest,' 'brains,' and the like.

My studies of Vampires, meaning the types of Vampires exemplified in all the lore, and literature of the age, met with varying degrees of success. I had encountered over the years, those who have called themselves Vampire. Typically, these non-magic Vampires, or Sanguinarians, would recognize Vlad the Impaler and Countess Bathory as part of their ideology.

Vlad the Impaler, of course, was the historical source material that one Bram Stoker plundered and sensationalized for the eager masses of his day. Vlad Dracula, it was understood, drank the blood of his enemies simply to evoke the proper response from anyone foolhardy enough to dare challenge him. That he was ruthless. That his ferocity knew no bounds. I emphasize: *not simply for the sake of drinking ones immortal blood.*

Countess Elisabeth Bathory, on the other hand, killed as many as six hundred women for the sake of bathing in, and imbibing, that most "wondrous" elixir, that dread "Fount of Sanguine Youth". Indeed, she believed that blood could stave off the harsh advance of years. She imprisoned and tortured women, like hapless cattle in her dungeons, and stole many a girl from her home . . . all for the mystical properties she believed were inherent of blood.

And here, did either Bathory or Dracula have knowledge of the primitive cannibals who believed, if they ate of their enemy, they would gain their strength? If they ate of their tribal vizier, shaman, or holy man, they would attain the sum knowledge of his life? Some of the human Vampires believed this and more. They believed blood drinking tapped them into auric energy fields that enlivened and succored them spiritually as well as physically.

In my wanderings, I had been alerted to places of alleged, 'true' Vampire activity. Nests, covens, basements of abandoned buildings, and such. But, I would invariably arrive late to the scene for actual, physical interaction with Vampires. I was basically left to only glean Vampiric behavior--and their thought processes--through their abandoned habitats. Very much like examining the cave drawings of immense antelopes, left behind by prehistoric man.

My one true astonishing lead happened by chance. I received information of a found object. **A Vampire's skull**. It was unearthed during the construction of an apartment complex in Denver. I procured this rare and important artifact from the son of a construction worker who first discovered the find. The construction worker informed me, to my horror and dismay, that the gift given to his rambunctious youngster was currently being used for a number of pedestrian tasks. A paper weight. A letter opener. Two hole punch. And staple puller! He even had the audacity to have adhered upon it . . . a psychedelic candle. The only reason why I was contacted at all was because the young man was experiencing nightmares. Apparently a modicum of smoke drifted off of the thing, and would torment him endlessly with its low, plaintive voice, way into the morning hours.

I visited the family while maintaining a guarded skepticism. Layers of doubt gradually weathered from my resolve, however, as I encountered the skull. In its presence I felt the most indescribable sensation. It felt 'right' in its 'otherness.' And the pronounced canines looked all too genuine.

But was it truly a Vampire's skull?

The evidence suggested that it was most likely a harmless, spectral manifestation attached with the skull. I discussed the possibility with the boy, and he confided that he had, at some point, **pricked** his finger on one of the skull's canines whilst . . . *pulling a staple from a term paper.* I paid the lad a rather handsome sum, as I feigned as much sympathy as I could possibly muster for him and his beleaguered condition. I offered him a vial of blessed water with garlic and parsley extracts, mostly for the sake of his enfeebled sanity. Carefully prescribed dosages. And I confiscated the skull immediately.

What happened as I took possession of the skull, and the following events thereafter, are exhaustively documented in my book **Vital Waters, Ruined Well**. How I administered a niggling amount of blood to its fang. How the skull started to smolder almost immediately with a thick cloud of arcane fog. How the fog fashioned itself into an ethereal face that clung and hovered about the skull, like the thin membrane of an enormous air sac.

And the first words it spoke, *"That boy,"* it said raspily. Feebly. *"That boy has a pornography collection, the likes you've never seen! They're like roaches breeding between his mattresses."*

"I hope he goes blind!" it said. Then it continued to moan, preoccupied so with its own fiendish agenda. *"BLOOD! Give me blood."*

I put questions to it directly. "Is it true that Vampires can control men's minds?"

The wavering face stopped short, as if stricken. *"You think you'd be sitting there asking me dull-witted questions, as such, if I could control men's minds?!"* it spat.

"There are no such things as dumb questions," I countered, "only continued ignorance, whilst in the possession of enduring and potent knowledge, with the power of drastic, and beneficial vicissitudes!"

Silence from the skull. Then, *"Eh, **whatever**. . .blood. . .blood. . ."*

After an hour of his miserable chanting for blood, I promised, if he were only to allow me an interview, I would give him his most life restoring blood. Reluctantly, he agreed. And over the course of three months, he offered me insights into the Vampire psychology. Even anecdotes and histories of his life and family, while he lived. Again, all catalogued and EXHAUSTIVELY reconstructed in my book **Vital Waters, Ruined Well**.

As for my encounter with the redoubtable Mr. Blassusos, let me say that it is best to describe the experience without flower, bathos, or imprecise metaphor. It should be addressed as starkly, and as uncompromisingly, as was the moment endured . . . and administered.

With that said:

8:33 A.M. I was in bed. He was standing over me whilst I slept. I woke, with a start.

///*"Pike,"*\\\ his voiced boomed a truculent tempo across my frontal lobe. It was telepathy. His lips hadn't moved, save to shuffle around his unwieldy fangs. He reminded me very much of *Odobenus Rosmarus,* the Arctic walrus, as grafted to actor Terrence Stamp. ///*"your book sucks! And I do NOT look like a bloody walrus!"*\\\

I was taken aback. "Um, uh, I'm sorry . . .! *Wait!* You've read my book?!"

///"It sucks! _You_ suck too!"\\\ Blassusos inspected my suite diffidently. Finding no chair, he perched himself at the foot of my bed.

///"Remember all the phone calls, those anonymous tips? You know the ones, '_I think I've seen some Vampires at the old folks home_', type calls?"\\\ he asked.

I nodded, like a feckless child, that I did.

///"It was a couple of me boys what did it. What set you up with a couple of red herrings!"\\\

My head throbbed as a stentorian laughter resounded throughout my addled psyche, as well as before me. His laughter rose out of his throat, as a hoarse, booming rasp that fairly shredded my eardrums into tingling bits of minute ribbon.

///"I don't like you,"\\\ I heard him say, as his laughter subsided. ///"You're like a lonely overzealous geek trying too hard to fit in with the 'In Crowd'! Mind you, we've been following your fool career, we have. Since first whiff. That's right! We smelled you long before the actual crap! You're a nincompoop and a horrible writer. You read like a bloody medicine cabinet!"\\\

His words were like a blow. "I–I," I stammered.

Blassusos rose from the bed. ///"That's why I consulted a total stranger. A writer I picked at random. He's doing a 'translation' of various secrets and such. I figure, it's high time the world knew what it was up against!"\\\

"You told someone else your secrets?" I felt jilted. Cheated. With colors paining my eyes, and brain, as palpably as hard marbles. The room swayed, as it slipped away into a miasmic whirlpool of–

///"*Strewth! Do you yap in your head like that ALL of the time? I mean, does it really come that naturally to you? Why can't your thoughts be simpler, without so much pretense? Keep it natural like. Think:* **'I feel like I'm gonna bloody faint!'** *Not all of that* miasma *routine, and drowning in a whirlpool of Whippoorwills, or some such shite! Who says, or for that matter,* **thinks** *the word miasma? You WALLY!?*"\\\

"Um! Huh! Uh, umh, uh-uh . . . yes. Yes! You were saying about secrets?"

///"*Yes, the secrets. The spells. All the spells.*"\\\ He said dismissively, as he moved to the window.

I was outraged. "To a novice? To an uninitiate?!" I cried. "He, as well as the work, will be famously dismissed by the academic community. By . . . by the world at large! The material may receive *some* notice if handled soundly. But, they'd . . . they'd never take **him** seriously! With some unknown mome attached to it, all will be for naught!"

Blassusos spun at me, his gaze settling on me with the oppressive weight of tumbled, mountain crags. ///"*I can get past the word 'mome',*" he said. "*Simply because I haven't sussed out what one is, right this minute. But you actually had the gall to use the word 'naught'? That just gets on my TIT, it's so pretentious!*"\\\

///"*See, you're acting as if you have a say in the matter. As though you're a part of the team. Part of the club!*"\\\ Blassusos swiftly, deftly, transshaped into an apparitional mist. ///"*They don't have to take him seriously. WE'LL take him seriously. But YOU . . .?*" The mist unraveled, churned, and gathered in on itself, ultimately dissolving through the pane of glass.

///"*Never . . . ever . . . YOU!*"\\\

Fourteen months later, I receive a rather sparkling, exquisitely drafted missive from the desk of one John Thomas Dimes. To wit:

Hey!

Got your name from a mutual friend. One Mr. Xxxxx Xxxxxxxxxx! Isn't he a holler?! An absolute SCREAM. AbsoTOOTly!

Anyway, I'm writing this letter as an invitation, yah know? Xxxxxx and I, we collaborated on this book thing. It's kinda cool, kinda casual. Very meat and potatoes. With a little pie and coffee afterwards, yah know?! Hah, I know you do. It really goes down easy.

Anyway, we got a publisher lined up, and we thought HEY, it'd be cool if we had you on board for the intro! Oh, it would be so GOLDEN if you could. Lookit, it doesn't have to be anything complicated. Couple of lines, really. Listen, if your schedule allows, I'll send you a copy of the manuscript to check out for yourself, kay? Drop me a buzz at the information listed below. Looking forward to it, dude.

Peace,

John "Ten Pennies, Two Nickels" Dimes!

Without haste, I scribed what I deemed as the appropriate response, for such a supremely affecting letter. Just as I was to post my letter, I received a creme-colored envelope, with just my name, written in a most elegant hand.

I opened the envelope to a wonder in script. I hadn't seen calligraphy that astounding, since I was but a young man, marveling at the awesome delicacy of an antique Chinese print, alleged authentic, as all Chinese artifacts seemed invariably presupposed–from the Ming Dynasty.

The lines of the letter I held were precise, and without fault. Smoothly applied, with a steady, self-assured hand. The words appearing about three quarters from the top of the page, a hair off center from the left. Large scripted.

The words, *"Do it!"*

Was our dear Mr. Blassusos extending this invitation as an apologetic hand proffered? Or had I been threatened ever so exquisitely? So seductively. Either way . . . how could I dare refuse?

I contacted Mr. Dimes, and asked that he send his little package along. Within a week I received the document. I read it, of course, with measured curiosity. And, it stunned me. Sickened me. It was everything I had hoped for. Everything I ever dreamt of writing. Of hearing and relating. I bore witness to the truth behind the fiction. All the long, dark histories of confusion had been cogently mapped out before me with a most beguiling geniality! The information swept me up like a great cyclone, and I was overwhelmed by the awesome dichotomy of change, and *revelation*.   My life was changed. The words effected my past, my present, and future. Yet, the world around me was not affected. And I knew, positively knew, that I would effect that change, as simply, and as easily as I lived.

Suddenly, "Shit!" The more I realized, the more I understood.

My position in the playing field of the sciences had changed. I was no longer distanced by the analytical abstracts of the Scientific Method. Where, like a demigod, I would orchestrate theoretical circumstances, catalytic environments, for a specific cause, to a specific effect. The most important part of the equation, *The Catalytic Environment,* that comfort zone of idly standing by. Of watching. Observing. Untouched, and untrammeled, by the events of the experiment, as it unfolded out onto its inevitable conclusion. This environment had been thoroughly excised from the scenario.

To put it in simple mathematical equations:

$X+Y=$ *Damned if they aren't as dangerous as I previously believed!* Naively, I entered into my theoretical studies of the Vampire as an 'intrepid adventurer', armed to the teeth with only cavalier pomposity, and 'knowledge' based upon blatant misinformation, and misdirection. In my hubris, I believed Blassusos had denounced me, and my work, for the sake of sheer, callous derision. Like running full tilt, **SWAAACK**, into a wall, I understood what I had not before. Simply by Blassusos' mere presence, and exhibition of power–*in the day time*–did he try to educate me, not deride me, in the errors in the state and affairs of my previous Vampiric reconnaissance.

A+B= Eddies _of primal terrors become torrential, sluicing wildly through me._ I knew I would know no true rest, would experience only a sick dread, feverishly unabated, until I barricaded my doors. Draped a wreath of garlic across my windows. Procured, and clutched the most ornate crucifix, or some other variety of magikal ward against evil, fast against my anxious bosom. And, of course, DRINK about a gallon of **Budweiser** (Not to worry. You'll understand my meaning soon enough). . .before the night fell!

10^{10}x10^{10}= I *felt bloody faint!*

And I did. Faint. And when I awoke some two hours (?) later, I gave Mr. Dimes a call.

He answered. "Hello?"

"This is Mr. Pike."

"Hey, Racey Boy! Howya doin'?"

"Um, uh uh, I'm fine. Fine thank you."

"So, whatcha think?"

My soul was a trench coat in the freezing rain. Icily brittle from frost. "It . . . it was quaint."

"Quaint?" There was just a shuffling sound on the other end of the phone. Like static. "Yeah. It is kinda intimate. Nothing I hate is stuffy, yah know?" he said with a guilelessness that left me undone.

I recovered my dignity, however secretly. "But, it was most entertaining. Wonderfully written."

"Cool."

"I must ask you, h-how are you going to handle your c-celebrity?" DAMN! What a lummox I was!

"You think it'll be a hit?" Mr. Dimes, asked.

"Oh, oh most assuredly. I think, indeed it will be a *hit*."

"Hope it doesn't," Mr. Dimes wisecracked.

"What? Why?" I asked. Grateful for the diversion.

"I tellya. I've had my share of minor celebrity. S'like owning a restaurant. People dig ya menu. Like your recipes. Change it the least bit, and alla sudden," Mr. Dimes voice became femininely affected. "*Chile, his food **NASTY!***" he said, laughingly. "Pleasin' a crowd, even thinking about pleasin' a crowd, leaves you no room for creativity. It Par-uh-LIZES!"

"Funny. All I've ever wanted was to be noticed. I can't recall a single moment when I didn't crave some kind of attention. The adulation for myself. For my work," I said.

I encouraged Mr. Dimes into another conversation, as my spirits continued to ache with its dire chill. "H-How do you feel about, about all of this, Mr. Dimes? The fact that Mr. Blassusos is a Vampire? Doesn't the fact that Vampires truly exist terrify you?"

"The old walrus, he's--he's good people! Makes a mean margarita!" Mr. Dimes let out a soft chuckle that rattled, and subsided raggedly against his fauces as he inhaled. "Hhm. Well, you've read everything, right? I know I should be afraid. Everyone who reads it knows I should be afraid. That *THEY* should be afraid. But, there's nothing to be afraid of, really.

"What is it, *'there's nothing to fear but fear itself?'* It makes so much sense. The only thing we, as people, seem to be afraid of is dying. Why? We don't want to hurt, or suffer, before we die. Because we don't want to give up life. I mean, all the work we hafta do in order to live. To survive. Even when you don't really want that much from life, other than food, and a' roof over ya head! For the simplest stuff, it's a hassle. And, more importantly . . . we don't know what'll happen AFTER we die! If we live with principals, will they be rewarded, especially after all the cool stuff we try ta do in life?"

"Yes. And everything we do, everything we touch, has been touched by the specter of death," I said, feeling very sorry for myself. And barely, hardly for the world.

"Hey? You know about ghosts, right? What do they hafta say about alla this?" Mr. Dimes asked.

"I'm sorry to say, my studies proved inconclusive. Some thought they saw a glimpse of the other side. Obviously the astral plane wasn't that promised land of Elysian Fields. It must be a bleak and fiery Gehenna, indeed, if they should want to hold on to life so desperately. Even a half-life, on this plane. So again, the fear of death, even in death. There is nothing after this. Nothing. Nothing but extremes of fear. Living from fear to fear! Oh, I--"

"Dude!" Mr. Dimes exclaimed. "Cut back on the caffeine!"

"Sorry."

"Lookit, you can get killed by a car. Bus. Truck. *Vampire*. You can even become a Vampire, but even they get killed. And that's the trick of it," Mr. Dimes said. "You can't concentrate on death, because it's, as you say, everywhere. You hafta not so much set up illusions to live, or rely on certain expectations, cuz alla that'll crack like an egg against brick hard reality! Ya haft enjoy what life has to offer. It's cliche', I know. But life--life is really a strange adventure. It *can* be an adventure. Ya can't think of life as something to do before you die. Or as an act of defiance against death. . ."

"Or, or being afraid to live," I reposited. "The old *'glass half empty, half full'* scenario."

Mr. Dimes got really excited. "Oh, oh, oh, oh! I've been saving this one up for *years* now!" he gushed. "The glass ain't half empty, or half full. The glass . . . just . . . *is*. . ."

His response didn't comfort me right away. My courage was likened, still, to a cellophane sheet. Flimsily insubstantial. I surmised that his simple words would be for me like an acorn nestled in the cold ground, waiting for spring. And years of sturdy growth. Years that would give a life volume, strength, and tough, mossy skins. Not callouses. Not even muscle, really. Just distance, and innumerable limbs for reach.

So here it stands. I'm writing an introduction to a book I wished I had written. And wished I'd never read. My life's work, and experiences, are but inconsequential wraiths, haunting the talents of the cunningly vital. And I say to you, dear reader, when you read this book, it will leave its mark. By all means, you'll be afraid to leave the house. But know, life is a journey. The destination? The destination is. . .*without doubt*.

Horace Pike

Wherever, USA, 2002.

///"Bloody Wanker!"\\\

THE
WHITE CORPSE HUSTLE:
A GUIDE FOR THE FLEDGLING VAMPIRE

DOCUMENTED BY
JOHN DIMES

1) I WAS MINDING MY OWN BUSINESS . . . REALLY!

I was visiting Seattle, Washington, one winter. It was around Christmas, perhaps a week or two following the disastrous World Bank protests, where people were actually selling used smoke bomb canisters and rubber bullets as Christmas items. Wonderful city, really. Engaging, friendly people, living happily in a parallel universe from the rest of the country. Overcast skies. Crisp, *'chill-you-to-the-bone'* air. Rain pelting you every other block or so. An inexplicable sunshine. Hilly streets that turned scrawny legs into wrought iron.

Coffee houses. Coffee houses. CofFEE houses. Clubs. Clubs.

And the Pike Place Market Arcade. A multi-leveled mall that looked as if fashioned from an enormous *serinette.* You know, those little music boxes that wandering organ grinder gypsies used to crank music from, while their little monkeys entertained and bilked people out of money? Very "out of time," with book and curio stores. Antique record shops, which also sold the cheapest costume jewelry around.

And, on the upper levels, outside of the market, in the dead of winter, you could see FRESH produce. I mean, vibrant tomatoes. Cabbages with that chalk of frosty morning on them. And the most startled looking fish. Like they're saying, "I was just in the water a minute ago, and now look. Just look, GODDAMMIT!"

At night I decided I'd find one of those celebrated coffee houses or bars of Seattle. I found this place called The

Point Direct Bar. I went in believing that it was karaoke night, but I got the dates of the occasion all wrong. There was no t.v. set, with flashing white lyrics across a blue screen. No people even thinking about looking through song books.

There was the low, boiling cauldron murmur of a lot of people, though. A 25 to 35 yr. old crowd, bearing a honey oats bread and marijuana coolness, about them. No one remotely pretentious. Just jeans and flannel. Sweat shirts, leather, and army surplus store jackets. And presiding over this wonderful, molasses casual atmosphere, was another kind of atmosphere. Sandalwood incense, covering, and failing miserably, the rank odor of cat piss (?!), and cigarettes.

I perched at the bar beside a lanky, dead pale guy, with blond dreads, who reeked warmly of Heineken, and sweaty flannel. I ordered a red wine, cuz I'm a wino, and admired the myriad beer rings that beaded and thrived undisputed across the bar top. 1) Because the bartender was <u>NEVER</u> going to wipe them down. 2) Because the bar had no less than twenty-five coats of blue paint caked upon it. The absorption rate was next to nil, it was so nonporous. Like glazed pottery, fresh from the kiln.

With vinegar in hand and Tom Waits' "16 Shells from a Thirty-Ought Six" jazzy, 'jumpGROWLing' in the background . . . I was happily deposited in an upturned corner of Heaven.

After about ten, maybe fifteen minutes of amiably igniting my guts, this old dude with a crown of white hair walked in. He looked to be about 60, but it was a life of excellent living kind of 60. Slender. 5'9", yet he carried himself taller. He was dressed entirely in black. He exuded a quiet elegance. An elegance that, obviously, defied his surroundings. And confidence enough not to give a good goddamn. After all, that's what money did. Set up the distance and the speed limits of propriety.

The way this guy surveyed the room. The way he had his cigarette pasted on the ledge of his bottom lip, like a disregarded spit ball, added to his 'matter-of-factness'. And, let me tell you . . . he was just pumping smoke. *Churning.* Puffing like a steam locomotive, he was. When he finally spied his destination at the rear of the club, he trailed smoke on back to a booth and was lost in a fog of his own, deep manufacture.

Frantically I broke out my notepad to jot him down as I saw him. I kept my line of sight as raggedly indirect as possible. I watched him as he rummaged up a dog-eared paperback from his coat pocket. His long index finger sliced to the middle of the book. As he read, his face broke up into patterns of incredulous delight and pained exasperation.

A handsome, disheveled waiter stood over him. The old man never looked up from the book as the boy took his order and was away in moments. I found myself totally stuck on the old guy, I was so intrigued. I wondered what his definition was. Who he was. What he did for a living. Did he <u>have </u>to do anything for a living. You know, all the nosy stuff.

The waiter sat two glasses of red wine on the table, and was gone. The old guy closed his book . . . ***and looked up at me.*** "BUSTED!" I thought to myself.

And without anger, he summoned me over.

JOHN: *Hey, I'm really sorry for the intrusion.*

BLASS: It's alright. Have a seat. I got this for you.

(He was referring to the wine.)

HAH! That's funny. Strange . . .

Having a bloke usher you over for a drink, in a straight bar? Yeah, that qualifies as strange. Don't worry, I'm not after your *ring*.

Hhm?

I'm not trying to get into your trousers. *'Ring's'* an expression for arse hole.

Oh, I get it. HAHAHAHAHAHAH! Hey, it's cool. What part of England you from?

London. Spent the last 25 years in Leicester Square. Had a little house. Sold it. Wanted to move on.

You're settling in Seattle, then.

Naw. Just passin' through. I'm on my way to San Francisco, then Hollywood. Hollywood intrigues me. Stars seem like such snotty bastards. Feel the need to take'em down a peg or two, yah know?

HAH!

Seattle reminds me very much of London. Only here, you get to see those spectacular mountains when the sun comes out. Winters in London can be rather flat. The sun is just as poached in the afternoons as it is in the mornings. The afternoon never rouses. It never seems . . . *likely*. Before you know it, evening has tripped over its own feet, and tumbled on you as sudden as a cripple! Name's Blassusos, by the way.

(He extended his hand for a shake. It was a good, firm grip.)

I'm John. What, um, nationality is Blassusos?

Greek. Family hails alla way back to Macedonia.

Cool! I can trace my family all the way to the ghetto!

Hah! That's rich, that! Hey?! Know where a fella can score a Mary Jane?

Hahahahahahah! Naw, naw. I'm just visiting like you. I'm from D.C. Back home I'd know where to go.

Yeah. There's this bloke in Bridport, Dorset, I know who could'a hooked us up, good and neat.

(I'm feeling real comfortable, yet uncomfortable talking to this Blassusos guy. Though the conversation was carefree, his body language . . . well. For one, he's chain smoking like a fiend. Rarely does a cigarette go out, before he lights the new with the old. I feel like I'm talking to God through the thick of a cumulonimbus cloud.

And his lips. Sometimes they looked like they were corresponding with what he was saying. Other times, not. I hear him crystal clear over the din. Then I can barely recognize a word. It was friggin' killing me!)

You a writer, hey?

Writer and artist. Right now I'm exercising my writing muscles.

What's your specialty, hey?

Well, I'm—um,

No need to get all bashful, like.

Well, I'm the typical comic book nerd. You know how people are about comic book people? If you don't know . . .

Oh, yes! I've seen them. Walking depositories of kitsch uselessness. With a sorta, wotsname . . . 'fanboy' glassiness to the eyes, hey? All besotted and polished up, like . . . like two blessed pearl onions. Just a bit of spittle at the corner of the lip, right?

Hah! Hey, I like you! Very, very cruel, that was! Very accurate, unfortunately. But, that's basically what I am to a certain degree. What I'm into. Sci-fi and horror. Horror, most especially. And, as you said, I'm a regular database of useless, arcane information. And what I don't remember, I gotta encyclopedia of horror at home. Actually two. And lots of books on the occult, just to keep things, you know, based in some kind of 'fact', right?

Right.

Wish I spoke as well as I thought I wrote, sometimes!

You're doing fine. Writing about me in that tablet of yours, were you?

A visual portrait, yeah.

Here. Give us a look, then.

Nah, nah!

Not nasty is it?

Oh, no, nono! Huh! It's just in the sketch stages. I'm particular about people reading stuff in its early stages is all. Any comment, one way or the other, throws me off. I end up chucking it, you know?

Hah! I'm sure whatever you have is better than whatever this one here has to offer.

I, um, noticed your disgusted look earlier.

Yeah. He's a real nincompoop, this one is.

*(Blassusos handed the book to me. It was **Vital Waters, Ruined Well: A Comprehensive Study of the Undead Mind.** I read the back, and looked up at him.)*

Ghosts? Zombies? Vampires? Hahahahahahah! He can't be serious.

Yep!

He's saying this stuff is for real?

Yep!

Crazy.

It only sounds crazy.

I'm sorry. You believe that this stuff is real? I mean, it's my business to believe in the surreal, just because I'm a morbid kinda guy. And us black folks are terribly, terribly superstitious as a rule . . . !

Hah!

But, I've never truly experienced . . .

Much as I hate to say it, some of it is real. Most of it's real. I've actually experienced Ghosts and Zombies for meself. I visited a graveyard once, saw what I thought was a funeral procession. When all the cars and people rounded this bend behind a tree . . . they vanished. I dunno much about cars, but they weren't contemporary. More like crank-up Model T's, like. Everybody all fitted out like Queen Victaria or some such!

FUN FACT: You'll discover as you read further, that Blass considers his graveyard recollections to be pure 'malarkey'. Which is to say, he saw what he saw, but it ain't what we think it is. He and I suspect that what he witnessed was an *Atmospheric Apparition.*

Atmospheric Apparitions are visual impressions, not necessarily ghosts that exhibit the essence of a strongly experienced series of events. There is the theory that quantum physics are involved with these particular brands of apparitions, that Atmospheric Apparitions are essentially dormant light particles suspended in the atmosphere. When variable environmental catalysts act on these dormant patterns, "the light particles vibrate in the atmosphere".

According to my friend Stephen Mera of The New Manchester's Association of Paranormal Investigators & Training (MAPIT), and The Scientific Establishment of Parapsychology (SEP), of which he is the founder, "The environmental catalysts are usually EMF, or GMF related. EMF being the Electromagnetic Fields emitted by local electrical pylons, substations, generators and household electrical appliances. And GMF which is the Geo-magnetic field that is emitted by the Earth."

Stephen also mentioned the concept of *The Stone Wall Theory*: "This is when old buildings such as Granite Stone buildings have anomalies take place inside or in the close vicinity of them due to electrical atmospheric conditions. Such conditions are mostly caused by the electrical discharge you get when pressing or crushing granite stone. Such charges can build up and discharge. At that point in time, paranormal phenomena can sometimes manifest." This explanation sounded very much like what happens when boy scouts start fires with flint. Stephen Mera was quick to agree with the analogy. (*Gee, I'm so smart!*)

So, the Stone Wall Theory explanation sounded right to me, since Blass was around all of those headstones, which most likely were made from what?! GRANITE!

Thank you!

Zombies. Hell, I went to Haiti. I've seen the dreadful bastards first hand. Them's pretty disturbing, even for the likes of me. As for *Vampires* . . .

You're gonna tell me they're real too? Now, I've heard of folks who like to drink blood, thinking they're Vampires.

Nah, not that nonsense! I'm talking the real bloody article. The Hammer Films, Christopher Lee variety of Vampire.

(Now Blassusos was scaring me. I was getting ready to raise up outta there, when he touched my arm.)

Listen, I don't like to be . . .

Relax, mate. I'm not gonna hurt you.

Hurt me? I'm a big BLACK mutherf#$% from Washington, D.C.! The murder capitol of the world, 25 years running! I got a hundred pounds on you! So, y-you better. . .

(I smelled the most beautiful fragrance coming from somewhere. Exotic and sweet. Like Bergamot mixed with roses. It was soothing, and incredibly hypnotic. Dazed, I looked around to see where it was coming from. Who was wearing it.)

John. John, I want you to look at me. And I want you to be calm.

(For some reason I was afraid to look at him. But you know I did it anyway. He'd stubbed out his cigarette, and had brushed the ashtray aside. The lamp to the back of him flickered, and sputtered with electrical shorts. The smoke drifted before him, again, as storm clouds passing. The shorting lamp added to the illusion of the micro-storm, as lightning.

Something happened with the smoke. It gathered, like someone had balled up clumps of yellowed newspaper. As

Blassusos raised his great, black shawl from his shoulder . . . the light shorted out completely.)

Hah, gawd!

(In the gloom of his corner, I saw that the smoke had compressed into two of the longest fangs I'd ever seen in my life! Briefly Blassusos' features expanded to accommodate the size and weight of his ponderous fangs. His mouth seemed immense. And his throat swelled to the size of a smoked Virginia ham.

By the time he draped his shawl back across his shoulders, the small lamp had relighted, he had a cigarette in hand, and he was surrounded by his signature nebula. His features were perfectly fine, as if nothing had happened.

I was startled.)

What the hell was that?! What—the HELL—was that?! That was the fastest bit of drama I ever did see!

Always have liked a bit of show, yah know?

What did you do?!

Odor Modulation. Gave you the old "Venus Flytrap" routine, just to lull you into a calm.

*(He pronounced "Odor" like a Bostonian would say "Chowder". **Owdah!** I would have laughed if I hadn't been so rattled.)*

I'm not going to get that "airplane glue headache", am I?

Probably.

What did you do with your, your face? And the f- fangs? Sweet Jesus, they're friggin' HUGE, man!

Well, you know what they say about Vampires with big fangs?

Huh, right! What are they, nine feet long, or something?

They're eight inches, there abouts. I can add about an extra quarter inch if I project them.

*Eight . . . ? Goddamn, are you prehistoric?! A saber-toothed Vampire? **"Australopithecus Vampirus"** or something like that?*

Hah! You are a bit of a nebbish to come up with that off the cuff!

All I gotta say is, with suckas that long . . . you'd have to make dinner reservations a week in advances!

Not necessarily. It's easily managed, obviously. Just the older we get, the longer the fangs.

Well, how old the hell are you then?

Very.

You're not gonna give that up, huh?

"Vanity, thy name is man," I figure. Wouldn't give you me correct age anyway. I'm the type that'll tell you I'm a million, just to hear, "You don't look a day over a thousand!"

Fine. But, where did you put all your, um . . . "stuff"?

Matter manipulation. Distributed all me cranial mass, and "stuff", into the rest of me body. What ain't in me love handles, is mingling with the smoke from me fag!

(I clamped my hand across my nose and mouth.)

Relax, lad. Got it all covered. And what I don't have covered, I can easily retrieve from your gullet, if necessary! HAH!

Hah, nothin'! And, and you've been talking to me . . . ?

Telepathically, for the most part. I sussed you have a bit of ringing in your ear.

Tinnitus.

Right. I figured it'd help the conversation flow better for you, over the noise of the crowd.

That's very, uhh, very considerate of you.

De nada.

(Once I regained my composure, I looked around the room.)

How—how come nobody is reacting? I mean, people must've SEEN what you just did! SEEN what you turned into!

HAH! I **'Strobed Reality'** a bit. Touched their synapses. Slowed the eye/mind comprehension. They won't be screaming bloody murder until next week Tuesday!

FUN FACT: Wedging The Mind: For those adepts with the facility of mind, where the spiritual ability to overpower, or influence, the tangible . . . with the intangible, unphysical, or the metaphysical . . . is a keen necessity.

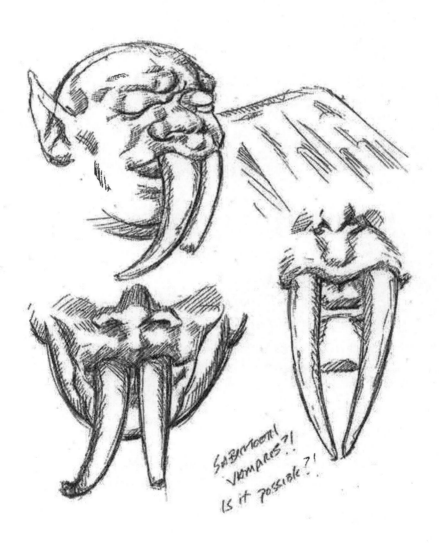

Bring this force to bear on the mind of your enemy, or those whose thoughts you would seek to easily, genially sway. It is a distraction, a void that one fills in an instant, with an instant or several instances. It is the spell of the conscious dwelling unconsciously on nothing or everything. An ouroboros cycle, fit within one, slim moment.

When, and where they remember, what you need for them to remember . . . is up to you!

-Blandite Opsky's: The Burden Manual

But you didn't do that 'Strobe' whammy, thingie, to me? Why?

I read your mind when I came in the door. You wanted to know what my "definition" was, right? What I did for a living, and all that? Here's your chance, mate. Here's your opportunity!

But why? Anne Rice has already, you know, written the 'definitive' interpretation of Vampires.

Buggery bollocks to that! Listen to yourself. That other stuff, that other stuff is fiction, mate. *Fiction.* I'm giving you the real deal, see? Not some Dickens tripe that inspires the masses to raid Percy Bysshe Shelly's wardrobe!

Actually, it was Polidori who . . .

(Ignoring me completely) Ascots, and cravats, with little jewels in them. Capes, for chrissakes! Eyes like Alaskan huskies! Fangs as small as the claws on a hen! And *S&M bondage*! What kinda malarkey is that?!

Well, I—

And unlike that heinous wight Rice, I'm only offering you a **ONE BOOK DEAL**. One interview and one interview only. If they're going to call you a hack, let them call you a hack but once.

HUH! Well . . . okay. What are we talking about then?

Spells, junior. I'm talking about spells.

Spells? A-As in magic?

Yah!

Why?!

God! You and your bloody *"WHYS"*? You're like an owl what spouts adverbs! Why, why, why! And don't look so bloody surprised I know "why's" an adverb!

Heh, well . . .

Look, I've been wanting to write a book of all the spells and conjurations I've discovered over the long years. Wanted there to be a book for the fledgling Vampire. There are so many out there that are lost, yah know? Having no idear where to turn, like. This will be that book. You can help me.

Why, (sorry) why me? Can't you write it yourself?

Of course I can bloody write it myself! But I'm a lazy arse, see! The way I sees it, it'd be easier to motivate meself if the piece was set up more as a conversation, like, over logging it down as a boring, formal textbook.

Besides, it's been my experience that people tend to retain information better when they're listening in on other people's conversation. And judging from what I'm seeing in that noggin of yours–well . . . I'm sure you'll inspire one hell of a conversation!

You remind me a bit of meself. You're one sick, curious bastard! Hahah!

Read that all in my head, did you? Well, I suppose I should be flattered. I suppose. But, but . . . <u>what if I refuse</u>?

Vampiric Telepathy
The Power of Unphysical Fiddling

Why are you fighting this?! You know you love the idea! What, you have control issues? Is that it? You want me to *beg* you to write it, when you know this little nugget is lodged up your butt, but good?

What are you, a proctologist or something?

Hah! Whatever! Will you please write it?

Look, hhm . . . I've got my reputation to think of. . . .

Gad!

Or my lack of reputation! I mean, if–if I didn't really wanna do it, what would you, um. . . .what would you do?

(Blassusos considered the question. Strongly considered the question. He smiled.)

Lemme, lemme tellya what I would do to you, if . . . IF you refused. I could swoop down on you. SNAP your neck like a crisp biscuit. That's "cookies" in American.

I'd drink your blood, clean as a whistle. *Right in front of EVERYBODY.* "Strobing" their wee little brains, all the while. They wouldn't know the difference, as I said, until next week Tuesday.

I'd hang your body from the ceiling fan, I would. Watch it wobble from the dead weight. And spin 'round like a labored pin wheel, with you dangled from it, like a long, fat glob of, of melted putty! I'd–I'd . . .

AAHAHAHAHAHAHAHAHAHAHA! You a damn lie!

Glad you caught on. I was running out of melodrama.

*(Writing a **Guide for a Fledgling Vampire**. Felt like I was making the most absurd decision of my life. Not necessarily the WORST decision of my life. If it got published, the most that*

could happen? Nobody, but nobody would believe a word of it.
People would think I was completely, "A-1," certifiable nuts.
Inspected by Inspector 12, nuts!

But, but, but . . . it could catch! And, I was actually
talking to an ACTUAL Vampire. Hell, I figured. Damned if it
wouldn't be a blast, whatever I did.)

Right! Gonna give it a go then?

Sure. Sure, fine! Got a pen. Got my, my pad. Let's talk.

Now, listen. I know you're bleedin' delicate and all right
now. Tender like. Because of all you seen. You need, mebbe, a
lie down, hey? Before the festivities?

Hahahah! Shaddup, Wanker!

Ah, you know the jargon now, hey?!

Heyyyyy!

2. THE TON OF BRICKS, OR THE FLEA:

Vampiric History &Schematics

This is the part of the conversation that I was the most geeked about, because I thought I was going to finally learn of the beginnings, the true origins of Vampire existence. Instead, I was faced with an even greater, more far reaching concept. Before me was the idea of Genetic Predetermination! The supposed *a priori,* non-external, genetic drive that governs verbal and behavioral organization. The static manifestation of the self before the self is even out of the box, folks! Sure, they say that even a body's sexuality is based in this predisposition of self, even though there were studies done on laboratory rats and fruit flies that suggested otherwise.

Well, it seemed that decreased levels of serotonin got a bunch of male fruit flies all randy-like. I mean HOT AND BOTHERED, folks. And they began "grouping" at the top of a jar, while a lot of angry female flies were down at the bottom of the jar going: "Hey, what's he got that we ain't got?!" As for the male rats, well, I imagine that there were some repeated viewings of the movie *Willard.* And, of course, when the scientists increased the serotonin levels in the fellas, they got back to the honeys! But was this increase actually fiddling with their innate behavioral traits?

Regardless of your beliefs on this issue, when you read this next segment, you'll make the same assessment I made. Vampires, like heroes, aren't made . . . *they're born!*

So, where do Vampires come from? You know, origins, and stuff?

Truth to be told, I'm not entirely sure where Vampires come from. What they mean in the larger scheme of things. Like the old story of the "Flea and the Brick."

"Flea and the brick?" What is that? One of those Grimm Fairytales I've never heard of?

Probably. But it's more like a parable. See, this flea wonders what came into existence first. His spare expanse of brick or himself. Well, he discovers that it really doesn't matter much.

Oh, I get it. Because all that mattered was the brick and how he spent his life, um--his days on it.

Nah. It's more to the point of the other brick that tumbles on him. Crushing him to death. So, it didn't matter what came first . . . as in what came after.

Morbid.

Just reality, mate. Simple reality.

So, it's not about the beginning.

After the brick. After you're bitten, there's a fifty-fifty chance that you'll become a Vampire.

You can actually be immune to the transformation? Even when you're dead?

Got this scientist pal that says as much. The cells circulate through the blood stream. But, they're dormant. It takes a bit of *'kindly'* or how did he put it? Oh, *"Cooperative Cells"* to trigger the transformation.

"Cooperative Cells"? Something in our bodies actually likes the idea of being a Vampire?

More or less. Listen. I don't understand it all, meself. I just know what the man says. He also says these cells are arcane, or metaphysical in nature.

Where do these magical cells come from?

Watch out for the brick, mate!

Okay, okay! How can a person tell if he has these types of cells? I mean, just in case he or she is bitten. So they won't have to worry about drinking holy water all day or something!

FUN FACT: "**Cooperative Cell** generation seems to be tied with individuals predisposed to having either strong psi ability or the resultant potential for psychic talent. While 'test subjects' were photographed by means of Kirlian photography, those that tended to fully succumb to Vampiric transformation were those that generated elevated levels of red and yellow in their auric fields. Red is the indication of energy, as yellow is the indication of intense mental expression.

"It could also very well be just a happy coincidence, and all the 'subjects' are just scared . . ."

-excerpted from the notebooks of Kerry Snod. Scientist/Vampire

Well, that's easy. Just get bit . . . *and wait.*

You've got to be kid–

Look! It's not an exact science. Just a recognized one. Me friend looked under a microscope, and saw this soupy, red "corpuscley" battle raging on. This "Magical Mystery Tour" if'n you will! He noticed a few odds and ends. That's that.

So this transformation kills you then?

Yep! That is, if you ain't drained dry first.

Cooperative Cells:
Yes, even in you!

Otherwise, a person without "Cooperative Cells" can survive a Vampire's bite and not turn into a Vampire.

Yes, unless he drains you dry. And mind you, a fledgling creature on "The Dinge" rarely leaves a victim full.

"On the Dinge"?

"On the Dinge", or "Livin' Dinge", meaning, your dead. Undead walking around, like. See?

I get it. There's a similar phrase in the gay community for white guys who only date black men. "Dinge Queens."

HAH! I've heard that one.

Any other colorful expressions? Like, what do you call your victims?

The "Spread".

Like in "eagle"?

nAH! 'Gutter-for-brains'! As in *"Your whole life **spread** out before you!"* But we tend to use another, shorter phrase, like: *"Hustling the Spread."*

Kinda has a football terminology thing going on there. "The 40 point spread" or some nonsense like that.

Yeah.

Also sounds like a kinky body butter or lotion.

You have GOT to get yourself shagged, Puppy.

Ah, I'm not that bad off.

3. **TRANSFORMATION: A Truly Helpful Time frame**

& Extended Schematics

The lore:

Once an individual is bitten by a Vampire, it usually takes three days for that individual to become a Vampire himself. This transformation is an obvious riff on the Christ story after his entombment. His resurrection from the grave after three days.

Oh, and coincidentally--it takes approximately three (3) days to suck that tough bit of gristle from between your teeth. WITHOUT the assistance of a toothpick, or floss, of course. . . .

So, how long does transformation take after you're bitten?

Two, three years.

Three years?!

(Blassusos' face screwed up in thought.)

Hang on a sec! Sorry. Hhmmm . . . it takes about a week, or so, for it to fully grab hold. Fangs develop in under a week. Bones hollow out of marrow, over the course of a month or two.

Hollow bones? Like a bird?

Fangs too. We're like walking cocktail straws. And just as pliable, we are. Because of our light weight, we can leap extremely high. Crawl up, or down walls, without much difficulty. 'Course, if you catch us unawares, a strong wind'll slap us against a wall, sure as swatting a fly! Or, we'd get blown every which way, like a bloody leaf! Oh, it's a mad scramble, it is.

I'm sure.

As for the pliability, the flexibility I mentioned. It's quite the Houdini trick, what we do. We can escape any confinement. Any restriction. Or we can place ourselves snug in any hole, just by performing little 'double jointy', yoga-ish kinds of shite.

Like fold up neat, and flat like a batch of freshly pressed trousers. 'Course, you wouldn't want to stay flat for very long . . .

Claustrophobia, huh?

Well, yeah, maybe a little . . . I'm talking severe muscle spasms.

Ugh!

The kind of agony you can only get from wriggling your pinky toe, seemingly past your foot . . .

Uh, yes!

Or when your leg feels like a pocket knife that just won't spring! The hamstrings, or calf strings, what-have-you, are nothing but stubborn, rusted coils of pain bending you into a helpless, friggin' midget, begging for sweet mercy!

Yes! Yes, I underst–

<u>Or</u> when you stretch your mouth past its limits, and it just wants to stay bent, and RAGGED on its hinges, like, in a stone, perpetual yawn! You can actually ***hear*** the muscle in your jaw, twanging all ugly in your ears like someone pulling a taut rope! The pain, the pain is . . .

God, yes, yes! I hate it, and I get it!

Hah!

Transformation time . . . <u>if you please</u>.

Yeah. Yeah. After all I've just mentioned.   After all the External/Internal Modifications, and all . . . you're wandering around like a maniac for about three years, regardless.

So, I stand by my original statement. Two, three years, proper is when you come into your own as a Vampire!

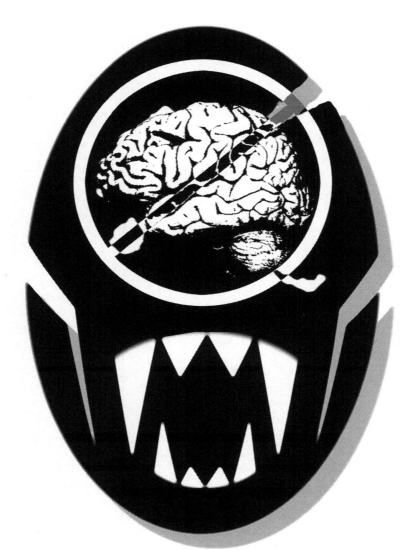

Vampiric Mental Collapse

Wandering around like a maniac?

You're basically brain dead, see? Sorta like a computer, shut down too long, what's taking its sweet time to reboot? There are some residual memories. Dodgy default systems, see? Eating. Sleeping. Walking around. Bottom line, though: your hardware is crashed all to hell!

Stop looking so damned surprised that I know about computers!

Well . . .

Got this friend of mine, mentioned in this book.

*(Referring to **Vital Waters**)*

Old Pike here gets this skull, see? A *Dingemen's*, um, Vampire's skull. Gad that got me so riled that did!

Pike killed him? Is that what happened?

No. No. Me friend topped himself, actually.

Couldn't stand being a Vampire.

Let *me* tell the story, hey?

Sorry!

Anyways! Pike gets a skull of a chum of mine. Good fella, our Jake. God bless him.

Pike gets his skull, and proceeds asking him questions, like. Mind you, we Dingemen never give up our secrets.

But,

Unless it's to our advantage. Telling Pike anything wasn't to our advantage. Detrimental, it was, to our delicate sensibilities, see? Pike's the kind of bugger who digs celebrity.

Pomp and Circumstance. A real name dropping, hanger on, kind of tosser! I'm sure his mother loves him, but we didn't.

Now, me and the boys, well, we got wind of this guy. Decided to wind him up with a couple'a pranks. Calling him up. Holding our nose, kinds of stuff!

How old are you again?

Hah! NO! You'll not judge me!

Hahah! Grown men. Grown UNDEAD men!

I know, I know! But don't tell me you've never had the urge to nick an old bird's purse, just to dump it in front of her? It weren't for the money! It was for spite, right? The old Shitz und Gikkles! It's childish! But that's the point, idn't it?

Yeah. Yeah, I get it. I'm always walking behind some white lady who thinks I'm going to rob her. So I just want to, you know—steal her purse off her shoulder. Then scream: "There! You happy now, goddammit! I stole your damn purse! Now HERE!"

(I slapped myself on the forehead.)

Dammit! You were reading my mind.

Right!

Quit it!

Relax. I'm respecting your privacy, more than you realize. Anyway, now, we'd call Pike up. Tell him that we saw some coven of Vampires at the old North Church, or some such. We'd trash the place! Scrawl 'ancient' hieroglyphs everywhere, in red spray paint.

Hah!

Even left used condoms!

4. **VAMPIRES HAVE SEX!**

Really, I never even considered the idea of Vampires getting it on. I mean, Vampires are usually portrayed as being these extremely virile, sexually potent beings. But, nine times out of ten, they ultimately turned into that familiar, rotting, fang-bearing corpse that roamed the night in search of blood. But we're not talking attractiveness here, folks. We're talking about Vampire sexuality. Dead on dead sex. *Menage a Morte'*. Necrophilia, but without all the judgmental, or illegal repercussions.

And, what of Vampire pregnancies?

I remember the folklore: If a Vampire looks at a pregnant woman, then the baby becomes a Vampire. If a Vampire bites a pregnant woman, she, and the baby becomes a Vampire. I'll never forget that comic book I read that had this story about all of these Vampires living in a lake. Oh, it was awesome! There was this one, ultra-rotund, female Vampire down there, who laid something close to like a thousand eggs. And there was a bunch of male Vampires swimming around, commencing to, you know . . . spawn. *Like salmon!* Oh, that was truly disgusting, and wonderful to see. But, at the same time, it didn't make much sense that a thing like that should work.

I mean, it was zombie pollywogs, swimming across deceased caviar, after all.

You left used condoms?! God, NO! Hahahahahah! Hey? Can Vampires actually have sex?

Blimey! I thought that one was gonna dodge right by you.

Well, do you?

Well, we can. Especially after a good night of hustling.

The White Corpse Hustle.

Hahn? I don't follow.

White corpuscle. Like in—

AHAHAHAHAHAHAHAHAHAHAHAHAHAH! Just made that up, did you?

Heh, yeah.

Use that for the title of the book!

Fine, but you were saying about sex?

Well, humm--after the hustling, the blood flow and all. Well, to put it mildly: It's harder than Chinese arithmetic!

That's pretty hard. But, from what I've notice, you said that you can have sex especially after feeding.

You don't miss a trick!

Am I to assume, since there isn't really any heart beating in you,

Gad, this is embarrassing.

Your, or to say, THE "Coital Hydraulics" are usually, how do you say—?

A mate of mine used to say: "For the most part, it's only there to keep the sand out of our fannies!"

Fannies?

Vaginas.

OH, HAHAHAHAHAHAHAHAHAHAHAHAHAHAH!

It's not THAT funny, you bastard!

Yeah it is! Hey, listen. I got you off your story a bit.

A *"bit"*?

You were discussing the skull. Your friend Jake?

Oh, right. Pike had me friend's skull. Pike is me least favorite cards in the deck. The Jack O' Ass, anna Ass O' Nine!

Hah!

He's lucky too. If it weren't for us looking out for him. If he had discovered the skull of anyone else. You know? Someone a little less gentlemanly? He would've been up "Sid's Creek", if'n you get my meaning?

I do. Book mark on Jake again.

Gad!

5. **A NUMBER OF VAMPIRES**

"Well, let me put it this way. If all the corpses buried around here were to stand up at once. . . .we'd have one hell of a population problem."

-From the movie "The Lost Boys", 1987.

I know, I know. Talking to you now, with all your talk about Dingemen, and stuff like that. It makes me wonder if, you know, you have rivals.

You mean Vampire gangs?

Yeah!

Yeah, sure. There's a rogue set out there. Sure. Just like everything else in life. You got some fellas who are just one of the old boys. Then you got some nasty elements. Sure. We watch out for them. Or, more to the point . . . we got our eye on them.

You've been giving out vague specifics. Saying things like "your mates", "your chums". And keeping "our" eyes on "them." Just how many are "We" are we talking, exactly?

Hear the brick?

Okay, okay! Just asking! But you've been doing a lot of dissembling, you know. But, really. Are you concerned that they, meaning this rogue set you're referring to . . . will read all this stuff too?

I, I mean, *we* . . . we are counting on it.

(I wanted to press the issue further, and decided against it. We had already established quite a trusting rapport. Didn't want to spoil it. But I couldn't help but to wonder, what could they, meaning his self-styled Dingemen, possibly gain by making all their secrets available to the enemy? And as for his reference to his buddies 'keeping their eye out'? I shuddered at the thought of Vampires taking good advantage of other Vampires during their helpless, and unfortunate, three years "Grace Period." With all the telepathy a full fledge Vampire had at their disposal, they could do some serious 'thinning -of-the-herd' action.)

6. SPELL/LESSON 1: ODOR MODULATION

How does one seduce, or draw someone to you? How, or why does one repel? In some circumstances, it is the surface appearance, in relation to the other's ideals of attraction, familiarity, or safety. For animals it is an instinctive process. Birds, especially the males of the species, with their wildly vivid colorations, or markings upon the plumage, draw the females to them. The puffing up of the chest, in instinctive, masculine bravado, that too, is the luring factor. But, there are degrees of yearning, yes? Layers that must be plumbed that makes the attraction, or the manipulation complete.

Ah, but what draws the male of the species to the female? Typically they are plain. Even UGLY. It is the scent. The pheromones! Women bear their own blossoms. Their own catalyst for lust, and excitement. We males, we males need our own advantage. Our own lures of certain bondage, that will not be denied, however our outward appearance, or countenance.

*Here be the recipes for **Odor Modulation** . . .*

-Blandite Opsky's: The Burden Manual

Jake.

Again with our Jake! Well, I'll tellyas about Jake, but you have to promise that you won't keep interrupting. Not for a while, at least. Turns out, his bit is important to the piece.

See, Jake has always been a good bloke. There's no finer gent. Dinge or Spread. When he was first brought over into the life, we kept an eye on him. Made sure his adjustment wasn't too unwieldy for him. Especially when he came to his senses, 2 or 3 years later. Didn't want him to have any regrettable experiences plaguing him, later on down the line, yah know?

Sure.

Took'em under my wing, I did. Kept him in a pen!

Like a dog?

Just like the family pet! Hah! Cleaned up after his mess. Let him hone his hustling skills all his own, right? Strobed him a bit. Gave him the Odor. The Ambrosia we call it. Put him back in his pen.

Left a pile of bunched up cotton swabs with the tincture of Ambrosia in it, like a pacifier for a fussy baby. Kept him nice and agreeable, like.

How do you make your, um, odors, by the way?

I told you no interruptions! So, shatyahole!

You said this is a book about spells! Start spelling them out!

Oh, yeah. Got me on that one, yeah. Okay. The creating of Odors is a relatively simple operation. Since the Vampire body is basically inert chemicals, possessed of potentially kinetic, alchemical properties. Like, say, salt and pepper? We go agreeably with everything.

You go, fool!

I'm impressed meself! Hah! Anyway, it's a matter of finding stuffs to add us to. We're walking recipes waiting to happen!

Like that whiff of Ambrosia I shot at you earlier. Concocted from a diet regime of roses, apple seeds, ginger, coriander seed, and bergamot.

Like in Earl Grey tea.

It's a process my friend calls a *'Homeostatic, Meta-alchemical Gestalt'*. Where all these dissimilar elements come together, creating something out of the ordinary. Something cohesive, and better than the sum of its parts.

Goddamn! I don't need to talk to you! Lemme talk to this friend of yours!

Up yours, you cheeky bastard!

Wait a minute? This Odor Modulation thing? Where, where is it coming from?

Oh, no! Getting all finicky on me again.

Please, PLEASE tell me it seeps out of your pores. Or, you burped it! I can handle a belch. Barely. But I can handle--

Hah! What an old lady! Hahahahahah!

Oh, why you laughing? Are you telling me you farted all that stuff? Farted in my face?!

You weren't complaining earlier!

Only because I didn't think it was another volley–

Volley?

That's the right word, isn't it?!

Sure.

Another volley of dust and stuff. Bits and pieces of your damned pulverized anatomy flying up my nose! I thought it was just a cologne, or perfume. Or, or, or . . .

Bathroom spray?

Yeah! **Air Freshener!**

What's a little broken wind between friends, hey?

Uuuuuhhhhh! Passing gas, no matter how fragrant, is just plain wrong, man! You don't fart in somebody's face! I don't care how pretty you can make it!

Relax, you great pillock! I'm just pulling your leg! It's produced from the pores. Hah! But it does remind me of ole Jake! Remember when I told you he topped himself?

(Grumbly) Yeah.

Well . . . oh, he's gonna kill me if I tell you!

I hate, hate, HATE when people do that! Don't start telling a secret then . . . !

I **want** to tell you, mind you. Just got to get past the ole failsafes, hey? The angst of knowing I shouldn't tellya, but wanting to all the same. Hah!

7. <u>**THE VAMPIRES OF DAWN!: Why Can't They Hack It**</u>

We've all seen it. Vampire is in the coffin. Antagonist waits for the sun to come out. Exposes said Vampire to the sun. End of story. Well, not necessarily the end. There is the suffering. The writhing in agony, and the explosion of bloody gore! Or, or, or, maybe there's flames! Flames everywhere. Oh, it's horrible what happens. But why? Why must this happen? Why *does* it happen?

Are the massive disintegrations of Vampires by sunlight attributed to natural, genetic deficiencies or are they due to arcane religious reasons? That they really are creations of the devil? Achilles, the Trojan hero was impervious to all harm, covered against all injury, except for his tootsies! That's a damned shame. The gods blessed him, but a lot of good it did him!

So if it isn't god or the devil, then what is it? Why is that unfortunate component left out of a Vampire's creation, where a little bit of sunlight fills the gap, and immediately addresses that neglected sequence necessary for their survival? Heck, we can ask these very questions about all life! Why we have to grow old and die. Why we have to suffer diseases. What I want to know ultimately is: Are these deficiencies in our natures-- Vampire, and human alike--accidental or are they all intentional!?

Whatever the reasons there are for all the things that threaten our lives, folks, it sounds to me that somebody needs to answer for it! That we all need serious refunds or some type

of spiritual, metaphysical compensation from whatever
Universal Insurance Agency there is out there, because they
simply ain't doing their job, I-tell-you!

See, Jake snuffed himself by accident. The way he explains it, he just come off a hustle. Went for a simple after dinner toddy. Some local pub, in Denver Colorado, no less.

Denver?

Jake liked to travel abroad. Anyway, he got a little pissed. Staggered down a hole. Sunned himself out of existence.

That's it? He got drunk, fell down a hole, and got burned by the sun. The way you were 'kee keeing' like a little Polynesian girl, I figured it was going to be something totally extraordinary! Hell, everybody knows that Vampires can't stay out in the sunlight.

Ah, Kemosabe`–but we can! Do you wanna know why?

Yes, I wanna know why!

Well, actually, it's a "how".

All right. How can you stay out in the sun?

You see, because of our diet, we tend to build up a lot of strange bacteria. And though we're not so much as decomposing, but inert. Well, whatever these kinetically/inert properties contain, the little 'micro-crawlies' just love it. And what they produce is what potentially threatens, and destroys us.

And that is?

High, I mean, HIGH concentrations of methane, hydrogen, and oxygen.

FUN FACT: According to the information provided by the Botavie Laboratories of Geneva, Switzerland, creators of an intestinal restorative product called *Deflatil*. *Deflatil*, I thought to myself, "Wow, what a pleasant name. Like totally non-aggressive in name, or purpose. A clever adaptation of the word "deflate", a gentle reduction in air) the compositions of intestinal gases are created by bacteria, yeast and fungi found in the intestines. These microorganisms in turn expel carbon dioxide, oxygen, nitrogen and sometimes methane.

Sometimes, sometimes these bacteria expel hydrogen.

HahahHOhoh! What you're saying is, you're one big fart.

Ever fart in your sleep?

Yeah, sure.

HahHAHAHAHAH! Jake, hehHUH, Jake was safe and S-SOUND in his little makeshift crypt, right?

Yeah?

Apparently he must've turned over in his sleep. Found just that one scrap of sunlight, see?

Cut a fart?

Yeah! HAHAHAHAH! He says he remembers there being a column of blue fire shooting up his bum! HAHAHAHAH! He panicked, and started this whole frightful chain reaction! He lost control, gassing it up some more! This time from his pores. Then POUF, no more Jake!

Hahahahah! So, in order to stay out in the sun, you have to cut a fart?

Several. But it's a total body purging session. Lasts about an hour.

FUN FACT Okay, everybody has always wondered whether their intestinal gas were actually indeed flammable. Everybody says (Who is everybody? Everybody is everybody!) that they've tried lighting their farts, but the results were mostly consigned to the world of folklore, along with Spontaneous Human Combustion, and therefore wholly ignored. Myself? I've never witnessed such a thing, but I still felt it necessary to investigate the matter further. As I mentioned, intestinal gases sometimes contain methane and hydrogen. Gases which are inherently flammable.

A little aside within an aside, intestinal gases usually burn either with a blue or yellow flame. Blue flames exhibit an active methane presence. I am to understand that methane producers are approximately 1/3 of the population.

OH, AND ANOTHER THING! According to my friends at the Botavie Laboratories, "People general produce 2 to 20 litres of gas per day, for an average 14 to 20 evacuation episodes (farts) per day." "However," they go on to say, "some individuals will suffer up to 140 episodes per day."

I just know there are a bunch of seven year olds (and some college guys) out there going, *"Cooooollll!"*

Sounds very Zen meditative. Wouldn't want to be ten miles of the place, from all the smell, I imagine. Oh, and the greenhouse effects you, and the cows of the world must be producing.

But listen, there is another bit what keeps a percentage of us wary of the sun.

Really now. Besides for the obvious?

Yeah. Hang on . . . how strong is your stomach, mate?

I'd say it's pretty strong. Why?

Remember those 'micro-crawlies' I mentioned?

Yeah, yeah. The bacteria, or um—bacterium?

Right, well, they are highly, what—? <u>Photosensitive.</u>

Like plants.

Yup, like plants. They can use sunlight to create food. However, because of their time in the Vampire body, they are like, mutated, see? I'm talking an accelerated rate of reproduction here. So much so that it produces what we Dingemen like to refer to as *"The Devil's Punch"*, or *"The Sunny side, Strawberry Custard Surprise"*.

Thuh-huhwhat?! The Strawberry Sundae . . .?

No, no! *"The Sunnyside, Strawberry Custard Surprise"*! Oh, it's frightful! Soon as they get a whiff of sun, the colony of crawlies spontaneously, and uncontrollably gluts the system. They got nowhere to go, but OUT, right? So, you get this viscous, 'mucousy', bloody SMEGMA pouring out of every orifice of your body. . .

Cough! Gag!

It's like EBOLA or some such! You're left all harried, and near to death. The symptoms are similar to a term I always stumble over in the pronunciation, but it's a simple enough abbreviation. It's called DIC. And it's basically how I've described it. Oozing from your nose, ears. Pores. Your *arse*. . .

Okay, okay! Goddamn. How do you get rid of the damned things?

You don't, unfortunately. Unless you stop drinking blood. It's the nature of the exchange. Obviously, the best you can do is stay out of the sun for long periods of time.

FUN FACT: **DIC** (Disseminated Intravascular Coagulopathy) is when insufficient clotting occurs. So, if'n you've recently had surgery, or cut, or some such thing like that, skin sutures, you start bleeding in enormous, ugly amounts without let up! According to my sources, there can also be spontaneous gastrointestinal, and genitourinary bleeding. In other words, you're a veritable geyser of blood from any and all orifices, or puncture sites.

Isn't that delightful?!

Mercy, that's a damned shame. Damned shame!

Yeah. But there are advantages!

What?! What the hell kind of advantages are there for turning into—into a raspberry cruller, crushed in somebody's fist?

Balls! I'm talking more on the line of the purging, in reference to fire, or flames!

Right, right. I see. Want to expound upon the virtues of being a walking Sterno now.

Ah, shaddup, you sarcastic git!

I tell you though, if you control it just right, it's like lighting a snifter of Grand Marnier. A little blue flame, coursing, say, along your fingertip, or your whole damned hand. Or launching it, like a dragon breathes flame! It's all about having a match handy, and a little mental precision.

8. **THE MATTER OF THE MIND OVER MATTER**.

They say that the mind can do the most amazing things. It can cause ones heartbeat to slow, and ones breathing to become so shallow, that anybody watching might think you were dead. The mind, they say, can even generate healing of internal, or external injuries. They say, that it can even slow the effects of aging.

Me, I can't even get my mind to remember what I had for breakfast this morning. But when I do . . . boy, am I proud of me! Uh, myself. I'm proud of myself.

This isn't terribly deep, is it?

Now, you've exhibited all sorts of magic tricks this evening.

Yes.

And mental precision, as you call it. Explain the process.

As you guessed, it's a matter of meditation. Concentrating on the entire body. And everything within it. Down to the last stray molecule. You have to be able to account for everything!

Sounds really difficult.

Yeah! And you gotta be totally sane to do it. Totally focused. Can't be half assed about it, at all.

Like when you turn into a fog? That's hard stuff. But, it becomes second nature over time. The fog trick is something you should never try straight outta the box. You begin first with making level sure that the brain remembers it has a body.

Huh?!

To use that computer analogy tripe, again. You know when you turn on your computer, and the printer, and scanner are off? And when you try to print something, it tells you, *you don't have a printer?*

Yeah, yeah! I know what you mean.

Right. You hafta to either turn the stuff on, and reboot, or go to that panel control thingie, and remind the damned computer that there IS a scanner in port 'whichie'. That there IS a printer in port 'thatie'!

Right, right.

The Vampire brain is a super computer. A **dead** supercomputer. You have to occasionally remind it that it has a body. It's like the whole body is asleep, you know? Like your foot goes to sleep? Can't move a bloody thing!

Damned shame.

Once that's all out of the way, you meditate. In tune yourself, with yourself. Then you can begin.

Begin what?

Stuff like plucking a hair. Seeing if you can get it to reattach itself to your scalp. Odor Modulation. Simple stuff like that. Then you can move on to harder stuff, like lopping off a finger, seeing if you can reattach it.

Damn!

Yeah! Once you do that, you can lop off the whole hand. See if you can move it around.

Hahahahah! Like Thing from the Addams Family.

Lovely! Exactly. Once you've got all that down, then you can move on to making yourself into a fog. And that involves, as I say, total focus. Like juggling twenty kabillion little balls in the air!

Does that involve your clothes too?

Hahahahahahahahaahhaahahh!

What's so funny?

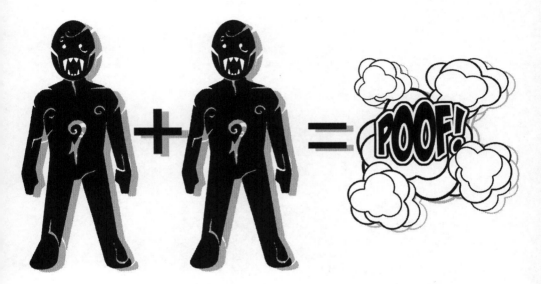

Vampiric Teleportation

God, you ask the most oddly appropriate questions! And you have no idea how embarrassing they are.

What?!

See, the secret to turning into fog, or turning into, say, a bat (which I'll explain how to do later), is that you DO have to get rid of your clothes, somehow!

That requires a simple spell of teleportation. You can find that in any reputable book of spells.

You'll give me a bibliography, I'm sure.

Sure, whatever!

FUN FACT: Okay, I was reading how this metaphysical scholar (Paul Christian, The History and Practice of Magic) tried to back up the concept of dematerialization with a biblical account of one of Jesus' disciples escaping from prison. Unfortunately he didn't say which disciple. So, I, along with Blassusos, went out and asked a priest. For some reason the father got scared and started crossing the air while shouting: "I abjure thee! I cast thee out!" Not since the Exorcist have I seen so much crying and carrying on! Ah buddy, what a flake!

Undeterred, I consulted my good church going Adventist friends. One said it was the Apostle Paul who escaped from prison. Another said it was the Apostle Peter.

"Well which one was it? How do I find out?" I asked them.

"It's right there in the bible somewhere, chile. . . .between Genesis and Revelations," one said.

I found out which apostle it was: It was the Apostle Peter (Acts 12, Verses 6-19) who escaped from imprisonment with the assistance of an angel who unshackled him, then ushered out of the cell and straight on past the guards. When the guards checked in on him the next day, it seemed to them that he had miraculously disappeared, even though Peter and the angel had walked right past them.

Okay. So. Why the big 'haha', then?

Well, as you turn into a fog, or animal, or some such, the clothes have to be teleported a couple of seconds before you transshape.

FUN FACT: The recipe for teleportation operates under the universal principle that no two like objects can occupy the same space and time.

With this said, fashion for yourself an astral body. Imprint upon this spiritual/mental manifestation the possibility, or capacity for flesh, thereby creating from it an exact replica of the self, or enough of an exactness that will convince the universal forces that there are indeed two like objects inhabiting the same spatial/temporal territory. Mind you, the ingredients required must be fresh. Or, in the case of the undead, i.e., Vampires, or any other such equivalent individualistic iteration--one must be well, and properly fed, for the undead are considered as Nihilities, or Inert Systems, by the universal forces.

The preparation for transmigration, or teleportation, when properly applied, will create an 'atmospheric causality', where all sorts of electrical chaos is produced, which is accompanied by a harsh, acrid odor, wherein, the original entity, over the replica, is stricken from existence, to land . . . ? In this case, a body will arrive at any point that they may have duly focused upon.

Here be the recipe for Teleportation . . .

-Blandite Opsky's: The Burden Manual

Hahahahahahahahaah! What are you? Standing there butt naked?!

For approximately a fraction of a second, you get full frontal. Or full dorsal, before we haze out the images!

FUN FACT: Regrettably, as I've previously stated, the preparation for full body teleportation cannot be effectively applied to things considered inanimate, or inert. And, as I've referenced, this includes the undead, Nihilities, Inert Systems, and the like. Any such beings who have not properly fed, or have not effectively rejuvenated themselves down to the smallest parts of their spiritual/physical corpus.

Clothes.

Clothes, keys, wallets, or any other such items, are obviously considered inert systems, and therefore cannot be transmigrated . . .

-Blandite Opsky's: The Burden Manual

Hahahahahahahahahahahahahahah!

So, hehHUH, so does, does every Vampire have the ability to do what you say they can do?

No, not all. Some may achieve only certain aspects, or levels of Vampiric power. Others are born duds. As in life, it's all a crap shoot, really.

And if you happen be one of those that can do pretty much every single spell, every texture of body manipulation, you have to worry about whether these abilities will totally overwhelm you.

(Blassusos got this sad look on his face, all of a sudden.)

What?

I'm reminded of this other bloke who got himself killed by his own magics.

Well, judging from the tone of most of our conversation, I wouldn't want to assume it was because he was overwhelmed by an excess of magical energies, and just yah know, imploded, or exploded . . . something like that.

Very good. He didn't. Nothing that easy, really. It was all psychological, actually. Psychosomatic, like.

(Instead of bugging Blass with questions, I let him settle in on the story.)

There was this particular bloke that was out after the spread. Looked quite dodgy. Torn clothes. Mussed up hair. Was mud caked, like he was aspiring to be Jamaican, or some such?

Dreads.

Yah, DREADS! Didn't have a bit of finesse about him at all. Still he'd jump out of shadows in a way that would hardly inspire whatcha call, *fear*, see. Just laughs, he was so pitiful. Had an odor that was furious as dung in hot, high summer. Still, had a definite knack for hypnotic mesmerization.

Ah.

Could inch the skirt up the most difficult bird, I-tell-YOU! Gimme a name!

Halle Berry!

Good as shagged!

Hah!

We weren't entirely sure who turned him over into the dinge set, because he was a difficult read. Most probably the other side. We'd reach in there in his head to see what we could. Jumbled, filmy mess that it was, it still managed a kind of cohesiveness, as a sort of automatic response. A natural defense mechanism against other Vampires reading his bean. It was like a layer of ice forming over everything.

Sounds like you're almost describing a frozen river bed.

Yah! We'd see the jumble of little fishies swimming about, but couldn't touch nary a one of them.

So, my friend Eggars decides, since we weren't getting any concrete answers about our fella's nature while in life, we'd best keep him locked down. Hopefully he'll turn out to be just one of the boys. If not, we'd handle him accordingly.

Of, of course.

Okay. So he comes out his initial three year, wild and ragged stage. He achieves clarity of thought, yeah? Turns out he's just a lovely lad. Laughs, jokes. Seems alright about being one of the dinge.

Then it happens.

Then it happens.

(Blass lifted a finger to summon the bartender. He pointed to my wine, and gestured that I needed another, and that he was having the same.)

What do you know about ghosts?

Hah! Ghosts, now! I know what everybody else knows. Or what they're supposed to know, anyway. The usual stuff. Ghosts are the lingering spirits of those who have died violently. Those that left this world with unresolved issues.

Right. Right. Go on.

Hhmm . . . there's also that stuff about precognition and post cognition, where people in the present are actually adepts, with the ability to see events that have happened in the past, or are actually still going on in the past, if you subscribe to the notion that all time is happening at once.

Load of crap, that. But go on.

Hah! Like I said, those with precognition, or at least the variety of cognition I'm describing that would explain ghosts, is the type of precognition where somebody is seeing events happening in the future, while the future is seeing them from the past. Which, of course, goes back to what I was saying about time, all times, happening at once.

FUN FACT: I read this alleged true account of a country doctor in the 30's who saw this ghostly image of a man, dressed in outdated clothes. I'm talkin' eighteenth century hunting duds. Top hat, caped over-coat, with a flintlock kinds of stuff. Anyway, the doctor sees the guy and apparently the guy sees him. The doctor checks his surroundings, just to get his bearings. When he returns his gaze, he finds that the ghostly gentleman from the past has disappeared.

Now, this psychic account was supposed to illustrate Retrocognition (Retrocognitive Clairvoyance) and Precognition, where the guy in the past was psychically seeing the guy in the future, while the guy in the future was psychically aware and attuned with the fella in the past.. The future seeing the past, the past seeing the future.

Like I said, MALARKEY. But, I'm seeing another idea in your head. The movie "Poltergeist".

Yeah, yeah. Poltergeist. Great flick. You've seen it?

Yeah, yeah. In passing. Sentimental, but interesting.

Sequels are a mess, but for the most part, the movie seems to dwell on the definite link between childhood behavior, and ghosts. Seems the raging hormones, or the psychic, spiritual turmoil of post adolescent teenagers, stirs up a hornet's nest of comparable fuss in the Poltergeist community. You know, bumps in the night? Broken dishes? Rearranged furniture?

Right, yeah.

(Blass was looking a little agitated. Distracted. It felt like he was stalling for time, until whatever the issue was became a smaller thing. Whatever it was, it was big, and big secrets tend to show its edges, until finally they just fall right on out, scrambling everywhere, leaving every one with no choice but to discuss that big, ugly thing that just fell on the floor.)

So, um—you're saying, what's name . . . that Carol Anne kid wasn't the cause of all that ruckus, hey?

Yeah, that's what I'm thinking. She'd be too young for a poltergeist to notice. Now, it might've been her crummy older sister who was the actual draw, the actual catalyst for all that stuff.

Now we're getting to me point.

Which is?

The older sister. More to the point, only the older sister, and not the ghost.

Okay, I'm confused.

Speculate with me for a bit, hey? You say raging hormones, and psychic, spiritual turmoil agitates ghosts.

FUN FACT: What my friends at MAPIT have to say about Poltergeist Activity: "The extra-ordinary and often destructive action of poltergeists is usually attributed to one person around whom the phenomenon focuses. This has given rise to the theory that poltergeists are either internally generated by people in a state of stress or that external discarnate entities are able to latch on to one particular person through whom they then act.

An adolescent (more or often a girl than a boy) is almost invariably present in the affected household, and this young person appears to be the nexus and attraction of the occurrences . . ."

Yeah.

Now, I've seen ghosts for myself. They're afterimages, you understand. Etheric, or auric entities, charged with the last bits of a body's memories. Folks are led to believe that auras are generated from people. In truth, they are holding us together. Auras are energy fields with consciences. Guilty consciences.

Why? Because they failed to do their duty? Keep a person from killing themselves, or being killed?

People are always talking about guardian angels, and such. That's rubbish—but only just. It's the auras, not the spirit of the person, doing the penance. They take on the burden until . . .

FUN FACT: I did a little reading, yah know! And you know what I found? There are references similar to what Blass is describing about 'guilty' auric fields, his version of what ghosts actually are. Well, the references aren't necessarily about guilty spiritual entities, but they are sentient outside human involvement, at any rate.

The Egyptian religion or mythologies, like the Greco-Roman and Norse mythologies, worshiped deities who governed or ruled over the common aspects of everyday life. You know, Thor for the rain and thunder? Apollo for the sun, and Gaea for the fertile earth kinda stuff? Omnipotent someone's created outside of oneself for praise and ultimately . . . blame. Leaving human beings free of guilt and all accountability.

Well, the Egyptian religion of antiquity not only believed in the outward, physical embodiments of life and power, but the inward expressions of these forces as well, as sentient spectral entities that resided within both the majestic ruling classes, right on down to the lowly, average Joe peasant!

Regard:

The KA: A body's "Doppelganger", or spiritual body double. Looked like you. Sounded like you. But far more powerful than you.

The AB: The heart. Primal instincts were said to be derived from the Ab.

The BA: The spiritual personage of the intellect. It fed you "common sense" or what seemed to be a priori knowledge.

The KHU: The often personified, spiritual life force.

The SEKHEM: Once again, a metaphysical personification of human dignity, strength and integrity. The quiet being that whispered of personal fortitude.

The KHAIBIT: Man's shadow. Was it evil? Who can say, really?

So, again, if these fellas weren't doing their job, it wasn't the human's fault! This follows the connection with all these spiritual entities. It seems that they could ultimately leave the body and actively converse with folks in the afterlife or heaven. Which more than suggests that these entities would feel they had a lot to answer for, and could be easily angst ridden over stuff should they let the KHAT, the Egyptian word for body come to harm or die unexpectedly

I wanted to tie these entities into actually parts of the human auric field, but some of the stuff seemed kinda redundant. But I couldn't help but to linger on the AB. Was the AB previously attributed with the Abdomen, the 'Ab Domain'?! You decide! And, um, terribly sorry for the intrusion. . .

Until what?

Who bloody knows!

Ahhhahhghghghg! You're driving me crazy!

Okay, the bloke I was telling you about, the derelict Vampire . . .

Yeah.

He comes out of his crazy spells, and turns out to be a good egg. He goes out, hunts the spread with us fellas. No problem. Laughs, talks. Can't get him to shut up, he's so friggin' garrulous, right?

Right.

But me friend Eggars, he says about our new chum . . .

Gimme a name. Just to get characters straight.

Right. *McLaren.* His name was McLaren. Me friend says of him: "He's a nice enough chap, but he works too hard at it. Laughs too hard, too long. Jokes too much."

"And that's a problem?" I says to him. He's says: "Like eatin' a flaky, shite filled pastry with sprinkles. First bite is delicious, but it leaves a nasty taste afterwards."

Oh, I've seen what he's talking about. It's real textbook. Sad people denying, or covering up the sadness with a lot of activity, or happy over emoting, just to cope.

Yeah, I've seen it too. But, but who's got bloody time to delve that friggin' sensitively all the goddamn time, hey? You pick and choose your enemies, and your mates. Confidants and castaways. Our fella, well—I just didn't want to extend myself that far out of the circle I've already established.

You probably sensed it would've been too much work, or something.

Probably . . . probably.

What happened, Blass?

He topped himself, he did. Poor fella.

9. __MAN, KNOW THYSELF.   NOW, CAN THEE LIVE WITH THE KNOWLEDGE OF THYSELF?__

Gnothi Se Auton. *Know thyself.* God, that's so easy to say. Those wacky Greeks were always so nosy, introspectively speaking! The truth of the matter is, some people just don't know to know themselves. And for those who do, it's annoying to know themselves, simply because they just don't like themselves. So, they essentially forget themselves. Sure, they remember to leave messages for themselves. Notes. But they seldom make time for themselves. Forgetting to take care of themselves. Or forgetting their own birthdays.

But the knowledge of oneself comes at you, as sure as that fleeting wave of broken wind in a long trench coat on a winter's day. As sure as that quick, pungent whiff of anti-perspirant failure.

You'll know yourself then. Oh, how you'll know. . . .

As I said, McLaren, on the whole, seemed like a pretty well-adjusted sort. Laughing, joking, the whole bit. But we didn't realize that there was trouble simmering under the surface, you know, like a pot of stew under a thick, fatty brine. You could only guess at what was going on. We'd ask him certain things, things about his life. We always got this sense that he was dissembling his information. Always dissembling. At times, we weren't sure if even he was aware of it. Always editing while he's talking.

It got to a point where we decided just to accept what the lad had to bring to the table, instead of venturing any deeper than was absolutely necessary. You wanna have your secrets, keep your bloody secrets, I says. No harm, no foul. He had a high caliber brain, didn't he? So we figures, absolutely trusted on instinct, that whatever idea, or grand pronouncement of the moment he had, was somehow grounded in good stuffs, yah know?

Yeah. Yeah.

Well, not to sound overly dramatic. Corny in the extreme, but, secrets for a Vampire are not like you average human secrets.

When humans have pent up frustrations, guilt, fear, what-have-you, it turns inward. You get your jittery nerves, high blood pressure, and your ulcers, and such. Totally wrecks the whole body, the whole system, hey?

Well, McLaren introduced to us a whole set of circumstances we folk never realized existed, where all of the unexpressed frustrations, angers, and what not, are turned inward, and expelled outward. These things, they, uh, they manifests themselves as shapes and images, like. Images that other people can *see*.

Ghosts?

Our version of them, at any rate. But, yeah. Ghosts. It starts off pretty slow, it seems. Like the conventional theory of ghosts. You set an object down, and it's gone the next minute. Ends up somewheres else. Sounds and footsteps. Thin veils of light hovering in the air. It looks like somebody, but you can't figure who.

That's amazing! You're saying that he, this McLaren character, was causing this ghost to happen?

Yeah, but, of course, he didn't know it at the time. Neither did we. We just passed it off as the real deal. That he might've been one of your, whatchalit, 'spiritual receptors', or mediums. Whatever. We simply told him to get a grip, and move on. Nothing to worry about. Especially in our world. The dead are going to attract the dead, in some way or fashion. It's inevitable.

So, it got so bad, these, these "visitations", they got so bad that it drove him to kill himself?

(Blassusos's winced thoughtfully, as though there was more to the answer than simply saying: "Yes.")

Yeah . . . yeah he snuffed himself. There's no doubt in my mind that he did.

Look, if you don't want to tell me. I mean, I can see that this is, this is totally--

Balls!

Me, Eggars, and McLaren, we were out and about one night. <u>We hunted the spread.</u> And afterwards, we wanted to be "civilised", see? You know, just to see how the other half lived, for a bit. Went to some pub called "The Shorn Lamb", or some such bollocks. Had a couple of pints. A bowl of crisps nearby, just to look all natural, like. Talked about **sports**, at the top of our lungs!

We later go back to the flat, on Leicester Square. Have another night cap, or two. And we're all giddy, like rogue priests at a cheeky lad free for all!

Hah!

Eggars goes off to the 'W.C.'. Apparently, like some stray cat, he'd acquired a rather resistant, or persistent, hair ball or something, from this hairy bloke he pinned down in the streets. He'd yet to wash the fine, Curly Que, 'kalumps' down, regardless of all his energetic swallowing. All the consumption of blood, beer, and crisps!

Laughter erupts from McLaren and I, like dust somebody just swatted from a dirty old carpet! I says to Eggars: "Are you sure it was his neck that you sucked on?!" Water was running in the bathroom. I heard him urging the little hairs out his mouth with that hock, scraping sound with his throat. "Kuh—kiss my arse, you worthless, whey faced, bastard!" I remembered him to say.

Lessee, I'm tired. So I says, to nobody in particular, that I was gonna have a lie down. McLaren pouts his lips like some fallen coquette, "Aww! Too early to turn in!" he says.

"No, no," I says. "Beer gets me all loopy. Need a lie down."

"Right, right," he says. "Be an ole spoiled sport, then! Off you go . . . *granny*," he shouted after me.

As I looked over my shoulder, just to give him a wry smile, I sees that he looks a little agitated. Wasn't upset with me, or nuthin. He'd forgotten all about me, at that point. He was just preoccupied, like. Like he was seeing things. Invisible things.

I'm in me room. Hhmm . . . threw me coat over a chair. Hung me trousers on the wardrobe door. I couldn't be bothered to drop me loose change on the bureau, right? Kept me shirt, and just flung meself onto the bed.

Sometime in the night, I feel this strange sensation. A tugging at me arm. Actually it was me wrist watch. It was eating into me wrist. Took the little bugger off, and made to set it on me night table.

The bastard flew out of my hand!

Where to?

Onto the wall, near my bedroom door. It wasn't the only thing on the wall. There was an old teaspoon that I'd had in the room. Couple a pair of gold trimmed cufflinks. Couple a silver earrings. A few metal buttons from off some really nice suits! AH! They were all there, crawling about, like glittering insects!

It was McLaren!

Got up to take a look. Plucked the spoon from the wall. Me grip went slack for a second, and the sumbitch rejoined the cast of "Silver Roaches on the Wall!"!

Hah!

Suddenly, it's all Quatermass!

Forgive me, "Quatermass"?

Ah, um . . . an old Hammer film. Gotta doctor, and alien bugs. Relies heavily on cheap theatrics. And even cheaper special effects. Uses a wind machine, and fake bricks during the *telekinesis* scenes. Look it up!

Right.

Where was I? Oh, yeah, I'm slapped in the face with me spoon and cufflinks. I'm knocked backwards by some invisible wind, till I hit the floor. This "wind" had some kind of grit to it that was stinging me eyes! I get up, and fight against the wind, while I'm blinking back the grit. It's very Chaplin, the way it looked. I'm leaning against the wind, and nearly parallel to the floor. Things were trembling on the walls, and the air, it, it had a mirage-like, rippled distortion to it. But it wasn't hot. It was unbearably cold, it was. Cold to the bone.

I hear sounds come from the dining room, so I struggle on in that direction. I look around the door frame to the dining room, and am startled by Eggars, who is pressed against the wall! "What the hell?!" I yelled at him.

"It's, it's McLaren!" he says. "It's his bloody ghost, I think!"

True enough, there was a gentleman hunched over McLaren, beating the crap out of him. Yelling at him, "Look whatcha' done, you heinous creature!" it said. "Nothin' but a monster, is what you are! An abomination!" All sorts of fire, and brimstone like that, right?

Whose ghost was it?

That's the million-dollar question, isn't it? Thought it was the ghost of one of his victims, tormenting him, like. But, for that to be, there'd have to be a ghost present. Remember I was telling you about ghost being auric energies, and what not?

Yeah, yeah.

There wouldn't be any, um, steady, or static lines. It'd be a undulating pulse sorta thing.

Basically you're describing fire.

Right. And there would be lights pouring off of it. Beads of energy would sweat off its skin, yet it wouldn't have any sign of real flesh about it. It would be like the movie of a person, shown on the back of a flame. Illuminated, transparent texture, I guess you would call it.

So, the thing that was on McLaren . . .

Looked just as real, and as solid, as you and I. That's right. And it turns out that thing that was on McLaren was his dear old Da. McLaren was screaming as much.

"Please don't hurt me, Daddy! Please!" His Da was pelting him plenty. Shaking, and rocking him back forth in his chair, while everything around us was rattling, like the air was boiling everything in a huge kettle.

I wanted to help the poor lad, but the force of that wind, aw—it was all I could do to hold on to the door frame, you know? I mean, the power, what-have-you, it had Eggars plastered against a wall, for chrissakes! He's stronger out of all of us, see?

While McLaren was being tossed about, I caught his eye. And for a moment, everything was calm. His Da vanished.

"Mikey? Mikey?" I called out to him. "You all right, fella?"

"Didja, didja see that?" he said. "That was my father. My father!"

Eggars and I went to him. "No, Mikey. No. There weren't anyone there," I said to him.

"You've got ta believe me! You saw it! You both saw it! He was standing over me! Look at me! Look at my face!" Yeah, he was a bloody mess alright. Eyes were near swollen shut. Mouth looked like bloody, flank steak. We're fast healers, we *Dingemen*, but his wounds would take a while. Or so I believed.

"He's come back," muttered McLaren. "He's come back from the grave, I tellya."

"What the hell for?" asked Eggars.

"He's always hated me. Always. Always . . ." McLaren's expression went all blank on us, as Eggars and I were thrown clear to the opposite corners of the room.

McLaren's father reappeared and just stared at him. Through rheumy, battered eyes, McLaren stared back. Looking back on it, I noticed that McLaren bore a more than passing resemblance to his father.

"Bastard, abomination!" McLaren's Da started strangling his son. "Monster! See how you like it for a change!"

It was like McLaren's most vivid nightmare was playing out in front of us, and there was nothing anyone could do! His father reared up, see. Sprouted fangs! *Fangs* . . .

My god!

He clamped down across McLaren's throat. Drained all the blood out of him in like, I dunno, ten, fifteen seconds . . .

Seconds?!

Yeah! That's how long it took for him to die. Fifteen seconds, give or take. And when that last second hit, Eggars and I fell off the wall, the room stopped vibrating, and McLaren's Da vanished. In his place . . . in his place was all the blood that had been sucked out of him.

With nothing there to contain it, no vessel, it just sorta *spilled to the floor*, as though someone had dumped it out of an old pail!

That's, that's incredible.

Eggars figures what occurred was, a combination of Telekinesis, Mental Telepathy, with more than just a hint of a Psychotic Break from reality.

Yeah, yeah. It all sounds kinda, Psychosomatic, doesn't it? I mean, the creating of his father's "ghost" through mental telepathy. Telekinesis for all the stuff vibrating, and flying around. The beating that he gave himself, essentially, not his father. The draining of his own blood from his body.

My god, the poor fella truly hated himself, and his existence.

Yeah, poor fella . . .

(BLASS looked haggard from telling me such a sad, yet amazing tale. Though he seemed purged, he still seemed weighted down, somehow. A tale that big, I figured, doesn't get smaller after the telling. If a body had any conscience at all, an event that traumatic is like the quintessential weed. You can tear it out of the ground, but if you don't get the root, it's only gonna grow back.)

Oh, Blass. You shouldn't blame yourself.

Hah! I don't bloody blame myself, Oprah!

Whuh, well, I thought you were sad because . . .

Sure, it's tragic that the bloke topped himself, and all! But the thing that's truly got up me damned nose is, that mass of grey, "ass backwardness" . . . the friggin' human mind! You think you know yourself, that you got it all covered, and the brain pulls all kinds of dodgy stunts! Who can understand it? Who knows when it's going to bloody turn on you, hey?!

And when your one of the Dinge, you never know what imaginary consequence, or cockeyed, telekinetic nemesis is gonna tumble out of your bloody noggin to cream you!

(Blass checked his watch.)

Got somewhere else to be, yeah?

Yeah, I do.

You haven't even given me that bibliography that you promised. You know, for all the spells and stuff?

Hang on, I got a pen here. I can scribble a few off the top of me head, like.

(Blass snatched up a cocktail napkin; scrawled a few fast lines. Pushed it over to me.)

*Hhm! Books on meditation. Um, what's this book here,
"**Blandite Opsky's: The Burden Manual**"?*

That there is the real deal. A genuine, authentic lexicon
of arcanity. Of deep, deep mojo.

*Uh, I see. This other stuff here on the list, seems like
they'd be pretty easy to find. Would this one be as well?*

Probably not. Only the best antiquarian shops would
carry such a tome. I figures if you're an adept, it'll find you,
over you finding it.

God, you even have a book here on Gestalt theory.

Again with the word Gestalt, hey? Important
information, that. When I first read up on the subject, it was
like being a self-taught piano player. You know how to bang out
the music on the thing, but when it comes to reading the notes,
within the measures--the, the language of musical theory, it was
a bloody mess! A whole new scope opened up to me. Stuff that
I had just taken on as instinct.

Mind you, after what I told you about McLaren, it
makes it all that much more, you know, relevant.

*Explain how Gestalt psychology is applied to everyday,
Vampiric existence. Explain Gestalt Theory period!*

Ah, Gestalt is, is the notion of independent elements, specifically the parts of the mind, that part that reasons, that part that remembers, and the identity or ego in the face of the external, are working together as a whole. When this whole, or 'totality' is at work, the mind attains attributes, abilities, functions that the individual parts would not normally, eh- exhibit on their lonesome, like.

Good googgedy MOOGAH! Go 'head Mister Psychologist!

Hah! I keep telling you, I only look, and sound rough and ugly, mate!

So, Gestalt Theory is basically trying to make all those things work.

Yeah. My personal interpretation is, that it's pretty much like getting your head out of your arse, see? Or hoping your head is out of your arse, at any rate, by attacking all of the things of the mind I just described.

It's simply about "common sense", and sanity. About knowing yourself completely. Your drives, and why you are driven by them.

You know common sense isn't always common!

Right. It's exactly as I've been explaining to you all night, the Vampire mind has to know itself, before it knows its body. And to do some of the stuff that Vampires are able to do, total control, total confidence, and total dedication to belief . . . *faith* . . . is necessary.

For example, I've been telling you about atomizing yourself, and bringing the elements together.

Um, you said it's like juggling a million balls in the air at once.

Well, once you've mastered that, the applications are as follows:

10. THE RECIPES FOR THE SPELLS OF MULTIPLICITY, AND ANIMAL TRANSMORGRIFICATON.

Do you recognize your own soul? Surely you must if you are to enact the spell of Multiplicity, and of Transmogrification. With this preparation, the soul unlocks many foreign doors within the self. Doors that can only be the mastered by the self. One must envision one's mind as a precise, 'golden skeleton key'. When this key is inserted, it should open out into, conceivably, overwhelming, yet heady experiences, potentialities, substances lent you from prior beings.

Be wary for they are only applications to be manipulated. Things not truly of the self. Not the self, yet within the self.

Multiplicity. Transmogrification. Here be the recipe for the purpose . . .

-Blandite Opsky's, "The Burden Manual"

The ingredients for the Multiplicity recipe,

Huh! It rhymes.

Shaddup! The recipe requires only this: Find a whole lot of ashes.

Ashes?

From funeral parlours. The ashes shouldn't be too fresh, otherwise the residual consciousness off of the stuff would be too strong, and it'll play havoc with your head. Which reminds me of a bloke who--

Is this a HAPPY story about a "bloke"?

Yeah, kinda, you ass! Seems the fella got his ashes too fresh, see? Woke up a couple of weeks later with pieces missing.

I don't get it?

The consciences were lingering on the ashes, see? His mind was enough of a catalyst to empower the once weakened thoughts. They took over, and took what they needed to survive.

You're telling me, that there are dead people walking around, created out of a Vampire's body?

Yep, that's what I'm saying.

What, what are these creatures called?

You find one and ask them, cuz I ain't never seen one. But they do exist. That's why it's important to get ashes that are maybe, a week old. Some degree of consciousness is necessary to use the ashes. It isn't considered inert material, then, but fertile ground.

So, that's all the talk about "native soil", and stuff, in Vampire lore.

Exactly. We control that bit of the ashes' mental, psychic fertility to our own ends, instead of it controlling us.

And when you get the ashes,

About how much?

It all depends upon what you're trying to do, which also involves default height, and weight. What you are, when you aren't something else, like.

With the Spell of Multiplicity, a spell that makes copies of you . . .

Copies? Why would you need . . . ?

To throw the enemy off. If you suspect that someone is on to your game, hey . . . then you lure them in. Let them think that you don't know they're there, see?

You let them follow you into your secret little hiddie hole, or crypt. What-have-you. Let them think they've caught you unawares. Then let them stake you!

But, it's actually a duplicate.

Exactly! You're working both your assailant, and the copied bastard, like remote control! And in order to do it right, to make that exact living, breathing, replica of yourself, you'd need your weight, your approximate mass in ashes.

Remarkable. But, what about, what about when you want to turn into the proverbial bat, or some other kinda animal? A wolf, maybe?

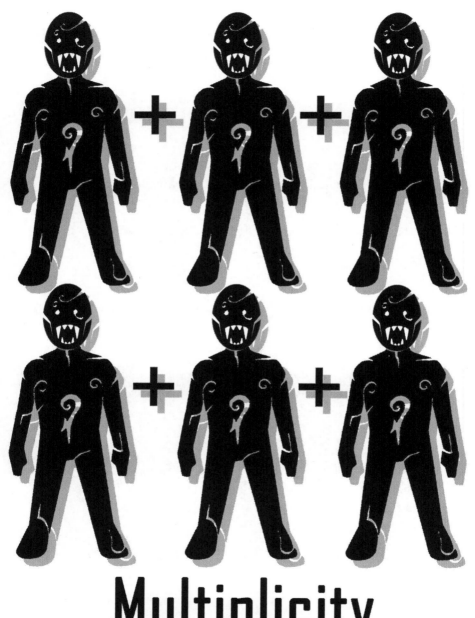

Multiplicity

Vampiric Transmorgrification
Accessing ashes for shape changing

Same difference. Burn up a bat, or wolf. Whichever animal you prefer. Incorporate the details into your body's default, and you can access it. Turn into the thing. And when you turn into smaller creature, say a rat, or mouse, your whole body doesn't just shrink into one, itty bitty, little mouse. That's impossible! At best, with all the mass of your body, you'd turn into a giant rat, or mouse.

God! That reminds me of Francis Ford Coppola's "Dracula", when Gary Oldman turned into a giant man bat!

Yes! I saw that too. That was an accurate account of mass distribution. Remember when the fella turned into a mess of rats? It weren't just one rat, but *several*. All, and every one of them rats were the parts of him.

That, as I said, is an accurate distribution of his physical mass.

When you say, "incorporate", what are you saying? What do you do, do you ingest it?

What, and make a spot of bloody arse tea out of it? Nah, you make a poultice out of it. Add a little water, just enough to make a sorta mud pie from it. Then you rub it on your skin, and wait till it dries. Let it absorb into the skin gradually. That's the best way to do it. Shouldn't flow around the stuff, atomize yourself to do it. Makes a mess that way.

Hah! I'm seeing a bunch of girl's in a locker room shower, spraying perfume; running through the cloud.

That wouldn't do at all either. But I'm not talking about getting ashes everywhere, I'm talking about if you swallow, or flow around the stuff, it doesn't give the old noggin time to register the new element, in its own time. Chugging the mixture down too quick makes the body rubbery, like you're a giant piece of untamed cytoplasm.

Sounds disgusting, but I gotcha.

Once the mixture is properly absorbed, it becomes part of your physical, mental default.

How long is this stuff a part of the "inventory"?

It's best to flush the stuff out of your system after a month, or so. It loses its elasticity over time.

Flush.

Oh, God! Where's your mind going to now?

How, hhmm . . . how do Vampires . . . ?

Do we go to the "Double-U-See"?

Yeah. I mean, essentially, you're dead right?

Essentially.

And your organs. There aren't any working in there, are there?

Can't say that they do.

So, how do you, "rid" yourself? Do you puke up your stuff like a snake, after you've digested everything? Do you excrete through your skin like . . . ?

Balls to that, you Wally! We like to refer to it as "grooming".

Grooming.

Yes! Grooming! God, you go such embarrassing places!

Well?

(Blass sighs.)

Go on, we're all friends here.

Let's just say . . . we Vampires aren't always terribly . . . "regular".

HAH!!!!

Vampiric Grooming

We don't excrete like your everyday living thing.   And we really don't have any bodily fluids, digestive fluids, and such. All the fluids we have, are, you know, 'borrowed'. And, whatever we borrow, drys out after a time. So we are in a constant state of replenishment, otherwise, we'd dry up like a river bed in the Mojave.   Solid as a rock. All this, and the fact there's no heart beating to circulate blood flow.

Oh, that sounds like some serious constipation problems.

Damn right!

So, how do you pass your . . . solids?

God! God, I--I, how I wish you would stop! Hah! Here I am, trying to create something bloody important, and you . . . ? You're like a bloody coprophile. Always concerned with what goes in, and what comes out, some poor old bloke's bum!

Ya damned right! Now, educate those poor fledgling Vampires out there that might be reading this, how to tackle a difficult problem! Or else, or else . . . I'll tell everyone in the world that Vampires can actually make Mr. Hanky sing--and dance--their troubles away!

Hahahahahahaah! Wanker! Bloody, bloody WANKER! Alright. We, well--we let everything get as, huh--dried out as it can, and we, um . . .

Yes?

We drop these little, crystalline thingies, about.

What, what are you saying? You crap diamonds? Is that what you're saying? Oh, HAHAHAHAHAHhahahahah!

Owtch! That would hurt wouldn't it?! Like I said, we 'groom' it out of us. While we're in our fog, or dust form. The parts that aren't animated by our mind, we let fall away.

I'll never look at igneous rocks the same way.

Ah, ya wee beastie!

Hah! Now, I know you say you have to leave, and everything, but, I want to ask you two final things.

Sure.

One is: Mirrors. What is it about mirrors that Vampires are so afraid of? I mean, you see it in the movies. It's always about evil can't face its own reflection, and stuff. Or, the fact that Vampires don't cast reflections at all. Which is it?

Once again, a lot of malarkey, that. Vampires aren't afraid of mirrors. And we do cast reflections . . . only it takes a while for our reflections to show up. It's like a daguerreotype slowly developing.

You mean those old fashioned, sepia toned photographs, with all those hook-nosed, Victorian matrons scowling away at you?

The one and the same. You see, according to my sources, Vampires are something of an optical illusion. A blind spot that can't be accurately picked up by the mirror. It's because of the way the light passes through us, bounces off of us, what-have-you, in relation to our constantly fluctuating forms, and wave patterns.

Whatever the technical jargon, a mirror can't accurately describe what the eye sees almost immediately. You ever see those picture done in reverse color order, like?

Yeah, I saw one of Abraham Lincoln, once.

Right. When you look at the image after a while, then look away, at say, a plain piece of white paper, you most likely saw Lincoln as he is supposed to look. It's called an After Image, I think.

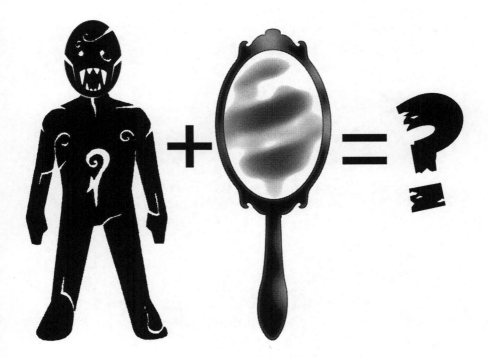

Vampiric Reflections
To be, or not to be.....

FUN FACTS: Facts About Mirrors: In order to reflect light rays without scattering or diffusing them, a mirror's surface must be perfectly smooth or its irregularities must be smaller than the wavelength of the light being reflected. (The wavelengths of visible light are on the order of 5 10-5cm.)

-From the Encyclopedia Britannica

YET ANOTHER FACT: Vampires in reference to mirrors. Simply put: mirrors are imprecise inert systems, facing *another* imprecise inert system.

-Blandite Opsky's: The Burden Manual

IS THAT . . .? WHY YES, ANOTHER FACT!: Afterimages: the lingering visual effects, or ghost-like imprint, left on the retina and other "associated visual mechanisms".

Sounds right.

It's a little like what they probably taught you in an art class, back in school. When you look at the color green, you aren't really seeing green. You're seeing everything BUT green. Because your eye is, um–starved for green, it translates green for you.

Okay, fine. Whatever.

Ah, skepticism. Well, if you happened to be combing your pretty, long locks before a mirror, and a Vampire happens to be creeping up behind you . . . you won't see them.

But . . . ?

If you sense that the Vampire is there, turn and see him, look back in the mirror . . .

Then you'd see him!

Yup! But the funny thing is, the image in the mirror won't be moving. Our actual image won't show up for another two minutes.

By that time, I'd be too occupied by screaming to notice!

Exactly.

What about photography? Can you be filmed, or photographed?

Well, hah–the only thing that'll show up is a lot of speckly nonsense. Like gas clouds in outer space kinds of stuff.

Well, there goes the idea having photos done of us together.

Ah, we can get someone to sketch something up, hey?

Okay, my final question.

Ah, you're gonna ask me about crosses.

Yes. Are Vampires really afraid of crosses?

Crosses work, if a particular idiotic Vampire believes it will. All about the conditioning of the individual.

But, if he doesn't believe, like in the movies . . . ?

Then you're basically waving a stick! Now me, I've been known to pretend a bit. Cringe away from a cross just to have the person come closer, so's I can . . . well, you know . . .

Yah, I'm getting it.

But, if'n you really want to do some true damage,

Ooooh, you're playing fair!

Hey, I'm a Vampire, not a bad guy. I'm trying me best to live right. Within reason.

Okay, what's the "true damage"?

Well, besides for the usual ways you can kill someone, I mean, like burning. You can always burn a Vampire, like you can burn a person. You can freeze us.

What about a stake in the heart? Or that beheading thang, or the quartering?

Stakes can work, but for only a few minutes. If a Dingemen is savvy, he can flow around the wound, and the stake. We're already dead, like. The heart ain't beating. You're simply nailing somebody in place for a sec!

But while we're occupied, flowing around the wound, while we're unawares, salt can do some real damage!

Salt?

Yep! We can't process it the same way as a living body, for some reason. Dirt and sand, is easy. There are residual consciences off of soil. Bugs, worms, and such. But, throw a little salt in the mix, and we're a mess. It's especially dicey for us that still likes to eat actual food. And we still have to shed the sodium after we've done the spread.

You're like a walking diamond exchange.

Hah!

FUN FACT: Salt, as in "Taken with a grain of salt". Or, a man is "worth his salt". Or a person is the "salt of the earth". There are so many variations on the theme of salt. It is the symbol of upstanding character, yet it is often the root cause of hypertension. High blood pressure. In the biblical sense (hah!) the apostles, as regarded by Christ, were referred to as the "salt of the earth". Yet, when would-be conquerors wanted to ruin the lands of their enemies, salt was often used to despoil the land; rendering it hopelessly infertile.

Salt was also used for purification, and for its therapeutic properties, for it was known that salt drew impurities out of the body. In the spiritual, or metaphysical sense, salt was the Tantric representation of the ego, as spilled into the Universal Self. Magically speaking, salt was recognized as having "white" magical power. You can get rid yourself of a zombie quick fast by feeding it salt, and it'll remember that it was dead, where it eventually returned to the grave. Well, hopefully, that is!

Lot's wife (Mrs. Lot?) was turned into salt, which again represents and embodies the love/hate relationship I'm sure anyone in her position would most undoubtedly feel for salt.

Now listen, are you sure that you want all this stuff written down? I've listened to everything you said tonight, and there is a common theme to all of this. It's all about preparation. Preparation for something. Against somebody.

That's pretty much what it sounds like, doesn't it?

Are your enemies that numerous? I mean, in this day in age, you can literally get away with murder, for a long, long time. With what you have at your disposal, you can easily blend in with the rest of the nutcase happenings.

Are you calling me a nutter?

You know what I mean. The damage you're capable of can be filed under the "bizarre" and "unexplained."

Don't you find creating a book like this is, you know, kinda reckless, or irresponsible?

Well, to answer your question about enemies. Without using all that government conspiracy tripe, I'll say only this: Just because I'm paranoid, doesn't mean they aren't really out to get me!

I know that's right!

SALT IS STRONGLY PROHIBITED!

As for the recklessness. I feel that it's important to have this book out there. There are a lot of the lost out there that would probably benefit from reading this. It's a combination text book, and a, um, history book. I, we, are offering those few out there an idea of their legacy. Their tradition, maybe.

Besides, I've thought of a few fail safes that you'll include in the body of the book.

Really? What kind?

You're gonna have illustrations, and photographs in the book, right?

Right, yes.

I'll give you a particularly powerful symbol that'll strobe, or scramble the mind/eye coordination, making everything look like bloody gibberish. Only adepts will be able to read the book without difficulty.

What about the percentage of people who'll hear about the book, look for the book, buy the book, and can't read it? They'll be wanting their money back in droves!

Don't worry about it.

What about finding a publisher? What if THEY can't read the damned thing! How will it get published?

Don't worry about it.

What about all these enemies you're supposedly paranoid about? Aren't there going to be someone in their ranks who'll be able to read it?

Like I told you before . . . I'm counting on it. So, don't worry about it!

(Blassusos got up to leave. I was literally vibrating with excitement. I felt I could light a cigarette with just my stare.)

So, where are you going? How will I get in touch if I have any more questions?

Haven't you been bloody listening, you Wally? Hah, I know, I know. It's too much to take it. Don't worry, I'll find you. I'm more than bloody capable of finding you . . . *anywhere*. Just get all the notes together, hey? I'll look them over.

CHEERS!

****

Blassusos stood up from the table, and with a dramatic flourish . . . he vanished before everyone's eyes. People blinked a bit. Collected their thoughts. And ultimately they felt it necessary to let out the most brain piercing screams. As for me, with Blass vanishing before god, and the world, I got what he promised. For a very brief second, I caught a shocking glimpse of what I thought was my dear friend's flabby (hah!), flabby pale body, and his—um, fanny camouflaging pudenda?

I sat there completely stunned, amidst all the commotion, and the lingering effects of that image burned--I mean **seared**--onto my mind. I asked myself the following question, "Is it possible for a person to die, I mean actually <u>die</u> from hysterical blindness?" Hah!

An Afterword by Blandite Opsky

I am elated that this tome has finally come into existence. Words, and thoughts are nothing, unless put to the page. Secrets important, coalesced into form are more potently powerful but for the act of its creation.   But realize, my friends--*my friend*--that there are sundry more iterations of thoughts that have yet to be explored. The thoughts themselves weren't unwilling to be expressed, it was simply the heart, as filtered through the thought process that had diminished their strength, as they fought to gain entry into this world.

Secrets? What secrets? Everything seemed to be explored here. No. The longevity of a Vampire. Blassusos never said, never allowed this subject to be broached. No, it wasn't because of vanity, as it pertains to the often heedless expression of years lived on one's countenance. Mr. Blassusos is actually pleased with how long he has managed to exist in this bright world (we'll narrow it down to a couple centuries, for even he has forgotten his actual date of birth), it is just that his age is also a source of great embarrassment. This double edged sword is one of the few things that he has allowed me to express here in these few paragraphs I offer to you, friend. He suspected, as does everyone, that the afterword of books are generally ignored.   A trifle that allows some famous, or infamous, individual to expound upon his own virtues, where he, or she is allowed to recount, and classify every nuance, every chance flower that should adorn the "regal" garland of his, or her, existence.

Let me say, my life is a dull one. I've lived for, wait . . . no. I won't tell you how old I am. That would take away from this moment. I will say, that I have had the pleasure to see all that there is to see, that is important to me to see. I have been privy to calculations, mechanisms, calibrations, that will allow me a few more years to explore all there is to know, when it is gone from the world, and sometime thereafter. Let my boast insinuate itself slowly, and make whatever bargain you will with the idea of it.

The secrets. Yes, Vampires can live forever. Vampires can manipulate their form, by sheer force of will, forever. However, the older a Vampire gets. Well, it seems that they have less control over how much matter they can contain. And how their appearance is perceived while in their human guises. Why?

The answer is insidiously simple . . . *shrinkage*.

When a Vampire reaches a certain stage of maturity, he begins to shrink. To condense, or compress. And this is not in any way remotely resembling the activity played upon those of the human elderly, as the waistline of the pair of pants are, ever so imperceptibly, hoisted across the breast bone, where the poor individual draws up as would a pill bug, because of osteoporosis, or arthritis. No, nothing as pedestrian as that, my friend.

The thing that occurs with Vampires is a process where the brain encourages the body to rid itself of unnecessary organs, or parts. The first to go: the circulatory system. Then, ultimately everything else is discarded upon the winds, like so much flotsam and jetsam. The heart. Kidneys. Lungs. Liver. What-have-you. All gone. ALL GONE. Why, even the parts of the skeletal structure are randomly expelled from the body. These deletions of the physiology occur during the sleep cycle of an unwary Vampire.   Sometimes, even when the Vampire is awake! Imagine, if you will, a compact klump of greyish soot seeping from behind you. There is a sensation of a subtle rip, or pull at you skin, at the base of your spine. Suddenly there is a soft, hollow crash as a stray bit of vertebrae is suddenly, and unceremoniously, flung to floor. And no matter how you try to reattach the offending article, it simply will not stay put. The brain simply won't allow it. "It doesn't belong," it says. And that's that! Oh, what it must be like to experience such an alarming thing! The only suffering caused, however, from these spontaneous subtractions of the self, would be incurred by the ego of the "wounded" party.

Not even the brain itself is immune to its own radical refining processes.   The brain is no longer recognized as two distinct hemispheres. It has now become a more economically structured thing. It is halved. And halved further still, until it is become a sleeker thing. After all, Vampires are essentially dead creatures, so why should it require those parts of the brain that control, say, the autonomic functions, breathing and such. It is deleted. And make no mistake, dear friend, though the brain is smaller, it is no less effective. The mind is now freer. It is more alert, now that it no longer has to deal with such trivial, or pesky matters such as blinking. Or coughing! Essentially, when a Vampire coughs, blinks--or enacts that rise, and falling procedure recognized as breathing-- it is for two reasons: 1) They are trying to keep in practice, and 2) It is a ritual ceremony in memorial to a thing that was previously always a given.

So, the body shrinks. The mind shrinks. That is what becomes of a Vampire. Regardless if they are transmogrifiers, or human/non-experimentalist. This is their ultimate embarrassment. And believe me, I have never helped in the cause of placating their bruised, and battered sensibilities. This is not due to any conscious malice on my part.

Simply put: When I first encountered the diminutive, or truncated versions of Vampires, well! I thought they were the much lauded sprites, or Leprechauns of Ireland! Of course, I had noticed their rather pronounced fangs, in passing. But it simply did not register.

Oh, yes! Speaking of their pronounced fangs. They are the only things that do not seem to shrink. Inexplicably, they tend to retain their original scale, in reference to the compression of the Vampire corpus.

Regarding the lives of Vampires, once they have become so small in stature. For a few of the human/non-experimentalist, the non-magic using Vampires, their lives are lived in seclusion. A seclusion far more severe, more solitary than the regimented life a Vampire has already established for themselves. They are forced to leave the big cities, in favor of small rural towns, for there they can live in relative obscurity. They reside in any grubby lodgings they can. They take full advantage of the wooded, mountainous areas, as an escape after feeding on those in the neighboring towns.

There are those, however, who remain in the cities. For these, their shortened stature is considered something of an advantage, as they stealthily feed upon whatever comes within reach. No longer are there the long, and laborious hunts for replenishment. The food . . . comes . . . **_to them!_** I am told that, many an unwary homeless vagabond, or conscientious sanitation worker, rummaging through a rubbish bin, have fallen prey to the wise Vampire!

And then, there is the variety of Vampire who shun the notion that their diminished size is a virtue. These hapless, and desperate few engage in an activity that is best described as _Prosthetic Body Cultivation._ This cultivation entails a Vampire turning a, hopefully, genetically cooperative human into a

Vampire for the sole purpose of temporarily possessing this new Vampire's body. As explained during Blassusos' and Mr. Dime's conversation, the fledgling Vampire's brain is quiet an erratic thing for approximately three years, which makes the mind highly tractable, or susceptible, to outside, mental manipulation.

When the mental faculties, and processes of the fledgling mind are effectively rendered inert, or dormant, the dwarfed Vampire houses itself within the fledgling, creating a beneficial, or symbiotic relationship. So, when the needs of the dwarfed Vampire's ego must be met, where he wants to stroll tall, and haughtily down an evening-shrouded boulevard, then he does so, and is sweetly intoxicated by the illusion of height, and limbs, that is lent, or borrowed from the fledgling. However, when the "needs most sanguine" arises, the <u>two</u> beings' needs are slacked, and sated . . . *not just that of the one.*

This relationship lasts until such time as when the fledgling has come out of its three year cycle of madness. That is, of course, if the dwarf Vampire is a scrupulous one! Blassusos, for example, has about a year left with his fledgling, before he goes on to cultivate his next. This is, yet again, another source of embarrassment.   For you must remember, Blassusos disclosed his "true" form to Mr. Dimes. And it <u>was </u>his true form, as generated across the face of his fledgling, at approximately four times his own actual size.

Now, there is one final bit of business that Blassusos has allowed me to address. The subject, for some, is of a prurient nature. Yes, yes, yes. I'm referring to intercourse, or sexual congress. Oh, dear, I may become flush. But he did want me to discuss it!

Vampires and sex. Well. They can effectively have sex with humans, as was described in minor detail within the pages of this book. However, sexual intercourse between Vampires. Ah, that's when things truly get messy. When you read this book, did you notice the absence of the fairer sex? Females, more precisely, Vampire females? Do they exist at all? Oh, but they do. The problem is, is that they must STAY AWAY FROM THE MALES!   Just as the males must STAY AWAY FROM THE FEMALES! Why? It's immediately simple: <u>Polarities</u>.

The average Vampire vibrates at distinct, etheric frequencies. Do you understand? They are like magnets, with opposite poles, and negative poles. But it seems, that ALL the males of the Vampire species vibrate at the same frequency. And all the female Vampires vibrate at their own, identical frequencies. So, when the sexes meet . . . things . . . fly . . . apart! My friends, I have seen this in action, and it is terrible! Oh, to witness people flying apart, suddenly, like dandelions before the rush of a whisper! It just shouldn't be countenanced. And it seems, that most of the males, and females of the species agree. So, when it comes to intercourse amongst the Vampiric sexes, well—well, to put it as obscurely verbose as possible: they become aggressively clannish; exclusionary to the extreme, and discretely . . . **they keep to themselves**.

Do with that what you will!

Thus, I come to the end of my part in the grand design that has been played out in this book. I hope, as do the authors, that this book has been educational, and enlightening, for the two are not always mutually exclusive. I also hope, and pray, that your days, dusks, and starry, constellation filled nights, are filled with an unsurpassed, and an unsuppressed glee!

Be in touch, my friend. Be in touch!

-Blandite Opsky

Acknowledgment and thank you's go out to:

Andrew Harmon. Carl Sublette. Richard Hnat. Terri
Allen. Pat & Cheryl. P.D. Cacek. J.L. (Judy) Comeau. Elizabeth
Richards. Maureen Nelson. C.W. Prather. James Fouts. Kent
Fordyce. Romel Chan. A. Ghastly Ghoul. The Carpathian & all
the Patient Creatures. Count Gore De Vol. Richard Dyzel.
Overton Lloyd. Everyone at Publish America. Stephen Mera &
everyone at the New Manchester Association of Paranormal
Investigators & Training, (MAPIT). Jacques Cardinal, Director of
The Botavie Laboratories. Anita Wolf, Senior Editor at
Encyclopedia Britannica. Blandite Opsky. Horace Pike, PhD.

Made in the USA
Columbia, SC
23 July 2018